I0795059

Troika

Praise for TROIKA

"Smith's prose is a crisp delight–at turns funny, warm, grim, sad, and joyous."

–The BookLife Prize

"In a voice at once fiercely honest and exquisitely tender, Smith explores what we inherit from our foremothers, what we pass down to our daughters, and the power we hold to forge new stories together. Like the best of road trips, *Troika* winds through shimmering vistas and surprising detours, delivering us, ultimately, to the possibilities that lie in our hearts. A wholly delightful journey from beginning to end."

–Nicole Graev Lipson, *USA Today* best-selling author of *Mothers and Other Fictional Characters*

"At its heart, *Troika* is the story of a road trip, but it's also a meditation on intergenerational legacies, memories of a left-behind homeland, and how coincidences stitch our lives together. Offering delightful twists and turns, Irena Smith delivers an eloquent (and sometimes humorous!) portrait of three generations of women seeking new insights about themselves and the sometimes complicated ways we carry each other forward."

–Elizabeth Rynecki, author of *Chasing Portraits*, documentary filmmaker, and podcaster

"*Troika* is a triumph. Smith deftly weaves her Russian upbringing, mythology, and motherhood into a tight, funny, and, at times, heartrending tale that will change any reader who goes along for the ride."

–Jen Murphy Parker, author of *Fault Line Boy*

Troika

Three Generations, Three Days, and a Very American Road Trip

Irena Smith

SWP

SHE WRITES PRESS

Copyright © 2026 Irena Smith

All rights reserved. No part of this publication may be reproduced, stored in a retrieval system, or transmitted in any form or by any means, electronic, mechanical, photocopying, recording, or otherwise, except for brief quotations in reviews, educational works, or other uses permitted by copyright law.

Published in 2026 by
She Writes Press, an imprint of The Stable Book Group

32 Court Street, Suite 2109
Brooklyn, NY 11201
https://shewritespress.com

Library of Congress Control Number: 2025927296
ISBN: 979-8-89636-108-4
eISBN: 979-8-89636-109-1

Interior designer: Katherine Lloyd, The DESK

Map created by Zoey Powers

Printed in the United States

Names and identifying characteristics have been changed to protect the privacy of certain individuals.

No part of this publication may be used to train generative artificial intelligence (AI) models. The publisher and author reserve all rights related to the use of this content in machine learning.

All company and product names mentioned in this book may be trademarks or registered trademarks of their respective owners. They are used for identification purposes only and do not imply endorsement or affiliation.

To everyone who left;

to everyone who stayed

Both Homer, and the sea–
'tis love sets all in motion.

–Osip Mandelshtam

AUTHOR'S NOTE

This is a work of creative nonfiction, and creative nonfiction is the practice of selective and imperfect recollection–which means that the events chronicled here are collected and retold to the best of my ability. Any resemblance to people living or dead is intentional; I've checked with the living, and they have given me their blessing. The dead keep their silence. The most improbable parts are the truest.

Part 1

POINTS OF DEPARTURE

January 5–6: Palo Alto–Los Olivos

Nothing natural or interesting goes in a straight line. As a matter of fact, it is the quickest way to the wrong place. And don't pretend you know where you are going. Because if you know where you are going, that means you've been there, and you are going to end up exactly where you came from.

–Naomi Newman, *Snake Talk*

The true risks of travel are disappointment and transformation: the fear you'll be the same person when you go home, and the fear that you won't. Then there's the fear . . . that you won't make it home at all.

–Kate Harris,
Lands of Lost Borders: A Journey on the Silk Road

Safe travels

The second time my father tries to give me a CB radio is in January 2023, right before I go on a three-day road trip to Solvang and Paso Robles with my seventy-seven-year-old mother and my twenty-two-year-old daughter in the midst of an epic storm. The storm knocks out power, uproots trees, floods streets, and brings down a pier in Santa Cruz. Meteorologists describe it in apocalyptic terms: bomb cyclone, atmospheric river, gale-force winds. A hiker films a water tornado off the Sonoma coast, a swirling wall of water rising from the ocean.

The storm shows no sign of abating on the morning we set out.

I saw a meme once where Odysseus announces to his crew that they're embarking on an odyssey. A sailor raises his hand and asks what an odyssey is, and Odysseus tells him it's a dangerous journey named for the only known survivor, and the sailor says, "Oh okay–wait what?" This is like that, but all three of us made it back. I was the only one who drove. I'm also the narrator, so I get to tell the story. The two are not necessarily related, but they're not *not* related.

If you already know we survived, the question is no longer *Did they make it?* The question is, *How?* The question is, *What are the stakes?* The question is–or rather, the questions are–*Where are they going and what's so important about this trip that it can't be postponed and what's up with the dad and the CB radio?*

Red sky at morning

My father hired himself out as an apprentice electrician when he was thirteen, after his father drowned on a beach picnic with coworkers. We almost never talked about my grandfather, but my father often told stories about working on huge ships and about growing up in Odesa, a colorful port city on the Black Sea where the neighborhood hoodlums relieved passersby of their watches by having a young child run up to them and say, "Mister, can I have your watch?" If the passerby refused (and the passerby always refused), a hulking man would step out from around the corner and inquire why the passerby was bullying a little kid. The hoodlums in his stories were comical and clever and only a little frightening.

He taught me to identify different kinds of clouds–nimbus, cumulus, cirrus–and to swim parallel to the shore until the current slackened if I was ever caught in an undertow. He taught me to ease up on the gas and steer into the skid if a car ever slid on a wet road. For as long as I can remember, we had a barometer hanging in a hallway or in the study wherever we happened to be living, and he monitored fluctuations in barometric pressure attentively. Once, a barometer fell from the wall and we joked for weeks about falling pressure.

My father loves maps and compasses and shortwave radios. He owns an extensive library of tools. He drops expressions like

"Red sky at night, sailor's delight; red sky at morning, sailors take warning" into conversations. I always assumed that he learned them as a result of rubbing shoulders with sailors and seafaring merchants while working at the port, but when I recently asked him if he learned "red sky at night" while working at the port, he said no. "Then how did you learn that?" I wanted to know. "By osmosis," he replied, and didn't offer any additional details.

In writing about my family, I have to resist the pull of what I assume is true, the siren call of what makes a better story. What makes a better story is not always true. Or sometimes it is true, but people don't want those details in the story. Or they don't want to be in the story at all.

Reservations

My father calls me the night before we're scheduled to leave. The rain is coming down in sheets. The roads are flooded. He thinks driving almost three hundred miles in a storm of this magnitude is a terrible idea and asks whether my mother and I might consider postponing the trip until the weather settles. I say no. He asks me if I'm sure, and I say yes, absolutely positive. We have hotel reservations, in Solvang for the first night and in Paso Robles for the second. There's a spectacular outdoor light installation in the hills near Paso Robles, and we have tickets for that too. I'll drive slowly and carefully, I tell him. Then I ask him to put my mother on the phone.

My mother and I make a plan: She will take an early morning train from San Francisco, where she and my father live, to Palo Alto, where my husband David and I live. That way, she won't have to drive in the rain, which makes her nervous. I'll swing by the train station to pick her up; from there, we'll drive thirteen miles south to Cupertino to pick up my daughter, and then the three of us will continue south to Solvang.

But on the morning of our trip, my phone buzzes. It's my mother, calling from the San Francisco train station. The trains aren't running because earlier that morning, heavy winds knocked over an eighty-foot eucalyptus tree whose trunk is now blocking the train tracks. It occurs to me that this is a bad omen, but before

I can say anything, she tells me that my father has offered to bring her to Palo Alto–an hour-long drive through a torrential downpour–and I say, "Great, see you soon."

He could have refused. He could have said, "This is ridiculous." But he ferries my mother to our house, and the two of them hurry to the front door, their heads bowed under the pelting rain. A wet gust of wind blows inside when I open the door to let them in, and they're barely through the door when my father hands me the CB radio.

How to get from Northern to Southern California

The first time my father tried to give me a CB radio was on a perfect summer day in 1987, when I was about to leave on a road trip to Los Angeles with my friend Leslie to spend the weekend with several high school friends who were subletting an apartment near UCLA. We were eighteen. We had just finished our freshman year of college, and Leslie and I were back home for the summer–she from Boston University, I from UCLA. Home was Sunnyvale, California, where we came of age in ranch houses built in the 1960s and attended Homestead High School–the high school in neighboring Cupertino that graduated two world-famous Steves, Jobs and Wozniak. Between the two of us, we had four years of driving experience, most of it navigating the few blocks between home and school, home and the nearby mall, and home (or school) and the Denny's at the intersection of Homestead Road and Foothill Expressway to have coffee and gossip and smoke. The latter was strictly forbidden at my house and passively tolerated at Leslie's.

We thought we were adults, but we were, in effect, babies. We were full of collagen and unearned confidence. We were irresponsible. We thought nothing bad would ever happen to us. We had no idea that catastrophes sometimes lie dormant for years, or decades, biding their time. We didn't know that we would drift apart, take different paths, become different people.

There are two major routes from the Bay Area to Los Angeles: the fast way and the scenic way. The scenic way (Highway 101) winds through some of the most beautiful scenery in California–the rolling hills along the Central Coast, the palm trees lining the absurdly blue ocean along Avila Beach, Pismo Beach, Santa Barbara, and Ventura County. The fast way (I-5) cuts through the sun-parched, dusty Central Valley, mile after mile of farmland and pasture and desolate clusters of gas stations and fast-food outposts. It's bookended by Pacheco Pass on the north and the Tejon Pass (which everyone calls "the Grapevine") on the south. In the middle, it's monotonous and soporific, the monotony broken up by flashes of terror while passing 18-wheelers at high speeds. Pacheco Pass was known to us as "Blood Alley," rumored to be haunted by the ghosts of the victims of head-on collisions and massacred Native Americans. The Grapevine was not known for anything except its long, relentless uphill stretches where cars overheat, its severe winter weather, and its ubiquitous semis.

When Leslie came to pick me up, my father carefully explained which buttons on the radio we needed to press to call for help and how to tune it to the same frequency that truckers use so that we could hear updates on road conditions. In the car, Leslie turned to me and asked, "Did you get all that?" I had not. I had, in fact, gotten none of it. Leslie hadn't either. We tossed the CB radio in the back, popped a cassette into the tape deck, backed out of my driveway, waved enthusiastically to my parents, who were standing forlornly by the garage, and lit cigarettes as soon as we were out of my parents' sight.

In the *Iliad*, Agamemnon sacrifices his daughter Iphigenia to the goddess Artemis hoping for a favorable wind that will allow a thousand Greek ships to sail across the wine-dark sea to Troy. He tells Iphigenia that she is to marry Achilles, and as she approaches the altar in her wedding finery, he slits her throat. Unlike Odysseus, who wanders for ten years after the fall of Troy, Agamemnon returns home smoothly and without incident. His wife Clytemnestra orchestrates a hero's welcome, spreads sumptuous purple tapestries along his path into the palace, ushers him into a bath, and stabs him to death.

I had not yet read the *Iliad* or the *Odyssey* or the *Oresteia* when Leslie and I hurtled down I-5 past mephitic cattle herds and fields of lettuce, smoking and blasting OMD and Springsteen and the Beatles. I didn't yet understand that going too fast could be dangerous. We didn't cover hubris in my AP Literature class, or maybe we did and I didn't remember. In any case, our safe return justified our extravagant carelessness.

I insist

"You know what they say about children and fools," I say to my father after I finish the story of that long-ago uneventful road trip. I make my voice extra jaunty, because inside I don't feel jaunty at all. "Anyway, we have cell phones now," I add. "And I'm pretty sure I'd be just as inept at figuring out the CB radio now as I was in 1987."

The three of us–my mother, my father, and I–are still standing in our entry. I'm itching to get going, but my father lingers, as though hoping that I'll change my mind if he finds the right words. My mother, who has been twisting the shoulder strap of her purse, says, "I'm sure we'll be fine."

My father has a rueful smile and a half shrug for occasions when he gives up trying to convince my mother or me of something. He smiles, half shrugs, and tells us to drive safely. Then he nods for emphasis and walks out into the rain.

If you're not home, you're in danger

Two months after my father was born, Germany invaded the Soviet Union, and two months after that, my grandmother Tsilya and my four-month-old father boarded a train crammed with refugees headed to Kirov, an industrial city over a thousand miles to the northeast. My grandfather was sent west to fight. My grandmother's parents, her two sisters, and her nieces and nephews were going to take a later train.

Then they disappeared. I always thought their train was bombed en route, but my father told me recently that no one actually knew what happened to them, that the train being bombed would have been the best possible outcome. He didn't say what the worst possible outcome was. One of the sisters had a newborn.

But on the train to Kirov, my grandmother, who was not yet my grandmother, didn't know any of that. She was preoccupied, I'm guessing, with breastfeeding and diapering and keeping my father from crying. When the train stopped, she washed out the diapers and strung a rope between the train cars and hung the diapers to dry. One night, the car to which she had attached the other end of the clothesline was uncoupled and went elsewhere, snapping the rope and taking all the diapers with it. After that, she claims, she trained my father to pee in a tin can. Whenever she talked about the war, which was not often, she talked about the indignity of that broken clothesline, the triumph of my father's early toilet training.

This is a story about a three-day road trip, and also a story about broken threads. A real-life clothesline snaps in the distant past and becomes family legend. Grandma Tsilya passes it on to my father, to my mother, to me; I pass it on to my children, this story about loose ends.

When I was growing up, Grandma Tsilya kept tabs on everyone's whereabouts. She liked it when we were home and worried when we weren't. If she called and no one picked up the phone, she would leave a plaintive message on our answering machine. She always said the same thing: "This is Babushka. Where could you be in such weather?"

It didn't matter what the weather was. It could be raining or it could be 72 and sunny with a light breeze. Weather stood for something else: unexpected catastrophe, chaos, people vanishing. "Where could you be in such weather?" had nothing to do with the weather. It meant *If you're not home, you're in danger.*

And yet

And yet it was Grandma Tsilya, who worried whenever any of us weren't home and who fretted about cold drafts and sewing needles getting into the hands of small children (needles were sharp and children were soft and vulnerable), who told my father to emigrate. My parents and I were visiting her in Odesa in the summer of 1975, and over tea my father launched into a litany of complaints about anti-Semitism, corruption, ignorance, stagnation, lack of opportunity–all the usual hallmarks of Soviet life in the 1970s. Grandma Tsilya listened, looked him in the eye, and said, "Then leave."

In 1975, her words were tantamount to inviting my father to walk off a cliff. There was no knowing where he and my mother and I would land, only the hope that it would be someplace better. If my parents applied to emigrate, there were two possibilities: Their application would be refused or it would be approved. In either case, they would lose their jobs and their Soviet citizenship as soon as they applied for an exit visa. The waiting period between application and permission to leave ranged from several months to several years, and permission was not guaranteed; some families were refused after spending months or years in limbo. Some were arrested. In the event that my parents' application *was* approved and we made it to the United States–an entity almost entirely unknown apart from carefully couched descriptions in letters from relatives who had emigrated earlier–there were also two possibilities: Our American lives would either be better than they were in the Soviet Union, or they would be worse.

A destination of our choosing

Like the English word *itch*, the Russian word *zud* has two meanings: an uncomfortable sensation that causes a desire to scratch, or a restlessness, an irresistible urge to do something.

My mother and I could have acknowledged my father's disquiet. I could have taken a look outside, where the wind was whistling in the power lines and shaking trees like a belligerent drunk, and decided that it wasn't worth it, and my mother would have agreed. We could have heeded the weather alerts lighting up both our phones that advised staying home except in cases of essential travel. I could have texted my daughter and said, "It's horrible out, let's wait until the weather clears or go another time." I could have considered the fact that if something happened to the three of us, my father, who had already lost so many people, might lose his only wife, his only daughter, and his only granddaughter.

Except this frivolous, ill-advised, unessential road trip feels essential. I don't know exactly what my mother is thinking, but I'm thinking that we're not getting any younger, that a change of scenery would do us all good. That the time would come when my mother would not be able to travel easily. That my daughter and I had never traveled together, just the two of us–at least not to a destination of our choosing. My daughter and I had never traveled with my mother, and quite possibly, I had never gone on a mother-daughter trip with my own mother. Going feels inevitable. We have to do it, come hell or high water (hell, to be determined; high water, practically a given). A look passes between my mother and me, acknowledging that although this may very well be a bad idea, there's only one way to find out.

We run through the downpour, throw our bags in the trunk, and duck into the car, shaking water from our hair. The rain beats an insistent tattoo on the roof. It's possible that before I turn the key in the ignition, one of us says *davai*, which, like *zud*, is a Russian word with more than one meaning. *Davai* means "give," but it also means "Let's go, let's do this."

Let's go

In the summer of 1941, my maternal grandparents–Grandma Ester and Grandpa Benya–fled Dzerzhinsk, a small town in Belarus, on the back of the last transport truck heading east, only hours ahead of the advancing Germans. My grandmother was nineteen and pregnant with her first child. Her parents stayed put because her father refused to believe that Germans–a civilized nation of composers, scientists, philosophers, businessmen who sealed deals with a handshake and remained true to their word–could be capable of the kind of brutality terrified refugees fleeing from the west were describing. My great-grandparents are still there, in one of the mass graves that was said to heave for days after the Germans shot the Jews.

My grandmother and grandfather sought refuge in a village called Mordovka. My grandmother gave birth there before they continued east. She had a difficult birth and tore badly and never received proper care. The tear remained. The baby died from pneumonia when he was two.

Bear with me

Instead of getting on the freeway, I decide to take Foothill Expressway to Cupertino because even at low speed, other cars fling so much water onto the windshield that I'm temporarily blinded every time I pass a car or a car passes us. Whenever this happens, my mother flinches and says, *nu i nu*, which is a Russian phrase expressing a combination of amazement and disbelief, similar to the English "well, well." The phrase is meant to be lighthearted, but there's a tightness in my mother's voice. She sits ramrod straight, her back not quite touching the seat back. Her hands are pressed together in her lap; she's wearing a big oval malachite ring set in silver filigree that she's had ever since I was little.

Taking Foothill Expressway means that the drive to pick up my daughter will take twice as long as it would have had we taken the freeway. It feels slightly cowardly, this choosing of safety over speed, but at the same time, I'm pleased with my prudence. Foothill Expressway, with its two lanes and regular traffic lights, feels more leisurely, less immediately dangerous than the freeway. It also takes me past high school landmarks–Lim's Chinese Restaurant, where waiters served alcohol without checking IDs; the Denny's where Leslie and I drank coffee and smoked.

My mother doesn't mind taking the long way. Seems relieved by it, in fact. She texts my daughter that we're running late, and my daughter sends back a thumbs-up. My mother and I reassure each other that there's no shame in going slow. Slow and steady wins the race, after all. There's even a Russian proverb to that effect: *Tishe yedesh, dal'she budesh*, which means "The slower you go, the farther you'll get."

My mother and I are almost to Cupertino, which seems like a good time to tell you that this narrative won't always take a direct path. It will loop and meander, detour and digress. It will require some patience. I am asking you to bear with me. I promise I'm going somewhere with all of this.

Cupertino is where my daughter rents a room in a house less than two miles from Homestead High School, takes community college classes, and works as a barista at a Peet's Coffee in the same shopping center that used to house the Denny's and Lim's Chinese Restaurant. Except that everything at the shopping center has changed. Lim's is now a nail salon and the Denny's has been replaced by Trader Joe's, and the fruit orchards that dotted the surrounding streets are gone.

Nomenclature

My daughter does not want to be named in this book, so we've agreed to call her NN, short for No Name, like the rapper. Or like the name Odysseus invents for himself when he is trapped in the Cyclops's cave. He tells the Cyclops that his name is Nobody, obliterating his identity and thereby saving his life and the lives of his crew. When we discuss this later, my daughter points out that moments after his brilliant deception, Odysseus shouts out his real name in a moment of impulsive bravado as he sails away from the maimed Cyclops, earning himself Poseidon's wrath and ten years of painful wandering before reaching home. We look at each other, unsure of what this means for our purposes.

I'm going to call her En for short.

En and I have a vexed relationship, because mothers and daughters are complicated. Because she and I are complicated. Because sometimes each of us wants something from the other that the other can't, or won't, give. Because En is secretive and I am nosy. Because the first full sentence she spoke was "I do it by self," and even though I recognize my own stubbornness in her, it's impossible for me not to interfere.

Timing

Ten minutes before we reach En's street, I adjust the defroster settings and ask my mother to text En to let her know we're five minutes away. En texts back, "Kk, be out in a minute."

En is not out in a minute. Or two. Or five.

I turn off the car and watch the rain pound the windshield. My mother leans back, examines her cuticles, sighs. Then she gives me a look that says, *Why is she like this and how can you tolerate it?* and I give her a look that says, *Please don't start.*

En was diagnosed with ADHD when she was thirteen. I was diagnosed in the fall before our trip, after discovering that the work-arounds I jerry-rigged in college stopped working. One of the symptoms of ADHD is time blindness–the inability to estimate how long an activity will take or to stick to a schedule. Another is emotional dysregulation, which, together with time blindness, caused operatic fights in the car every morning when En was in high school and working from the assumption that we could leave our house at 8:12 a.m. and arrive at school on time for first period, which started at 8:15 a.m.–even though it was a well-established fact that it took at least twelve minutes to get to school *even if all the lights were green and there was no traffic.*

My mother's phone pings with another text from En. The text says, "Two more minutes! I'll be right out!" I say, "My guess is that she's looking for something." My mother says nothing and sighs again.

Twelve minutes after texting that she needed two more minutes, En emerges from the house and runs through the rain. She's carrying a half-zipped duffel bag and an energy drink; a backpack swings from her shoulder. "Oopsie poopsie, sorry I'm late!" she calls out cheerfully as she opens the car door. "Let's get outta here!"

Landmarks

The purpose of our trip is to see an outdoor light installation in the hills near Paso Robles on California's Central Coast. At the last minute, my mother and I look at a map and decide that since we're already driving south, we may as well tack on a night in Solvang, a quaint Dutch village a hundred miles south of Paso Robles. Our reasoning is based largely on the fact that decades ago, Grandma Tsilya and Grandma Ester visited Solvang on a bus tour of Central and Southern California and came back raving about the adorable little town with windmills and wood-timbered houses with thatched roofs and tiny, delectable pancakes shaped like spheres. My mother and I have never been to Solvang, and neither has En.

The visit to Paso Robles, on the other hand, has been in the making since spring 2019, after I read about artist Bruce Munro's Field of Light, an immersive light installation set in the hills outside Paso Robles. Tens of thousands of stemmed fiber-optic spheres, spread across fifteen undulating acres, blooming to life when night fell. My husband David and I made plans to see it in April 2020 to celebrate our thirtieth anniversary; separately, my parents made plans to bring En to Paso Robles later that summer.

But instead of admiring the lights, David and En and I hunkered down at home, disinfecting groceries and tracking local

COVID cases. Two weeks into lockdown, En took a pill laced with fentanyl and almost died.

I rode with her in the ambulance and got sent away as soon as we got to the hospital, in accordance with COVID protocols, so I walked the seven miles home because I didn't want to see or talk to anyone, not even David. The streets were familiar, but I could no longer recognize my own life.

Entrances and exits

The on-ramp to southbound 85 is partly flooded. My mother is telling En about the blocked train tracks and En is saying, "No way!" and I say, "Ha ha, exactly" as I maneuver cautiously onto the freeway. The right lane is also partly flooded, and I merge left so I won't have to drive through the standing water, and once we're safely in the second-to-right lane, I yell, "Road trip!" From the back seat, En echoes, "Road trip!" My mother shakes both fists above her head triumphantly and cheers, but she is canted forward, scanning the road for hazards.

Traffic is crawling. Visibility is nearly zero. After approximately two miles, I ask if anyone is interested in stopping for coffee. My mother and En are both interested, so we exit the freeway in Saratoga, a small hillside town, and head toward downtown, and I say that even with terrible weather and snail-slow progress, there's just something about being on a road trip.

Terra incognita

Medieval cartographers wrote *hic sunt dracones* on the edges of the maps where the known world ended. "Here be dragons"–proceed at your own risk. But the books of my childhood lured me to those edges. Pushkin's *Ruslan i Lyudmila*, with its catalog of enchantments–an oak growing by the seashore, a learned cat that told stories and sang songs, forest spirits and villains who abducted maidens, a witch who lived in a windowless, doorless hut on chicken legs. *The Tale of Tsar Saltan*–jealousy, magic, betrayal, loyalty, a young mother and babe sealed in a barrel and set adrift on the sea, their miraculous survival. A children's edition of Harriet Tubman's biography. Jack London, Fenimore Cooper, Jules Verne. Travels by balloon, travels by boat, travels by foot, travels to the center of the earth, travels twenty thousand leagues under the sea.

When I was seven, I discovered a book in my parents' home library called *Odnoetazhnaya Amerika.* Translated literally, *Odnoetazhnaya Amerika* means *One-Story America* or *Single-Story America*, which is confusing because in English, a "story" might refer either to a narrative or to the levels of a building. The Russian title is unambiguous; it refers to the one and only level of a building that you can see from a moving car. Let's call it *Roadside America.*

Roadside America is an account of a 1930s cross-country American road trip undertaken by Ilya Ilf and Evgeniy Petrov, two

Soviet writers who received unprecedented permission from the Soviet government to travel to the United States in 1936 and chronicle their coast-to-coast journey. They bought a car and enlisted a Russian-speaking American couple, Mr. and Mrs. Adams, to accompany them. Mrs. Adams–stoic and largely silent–drove; Mr. Adams–voluble, curious, childlike, fumbling, forgetful–developed the itinerary, served as a translator, and provided colorful commentary and comic relief.

The book's authors met in the 1920s while writing for a Soviet literary magazine and quickly became friends and collaborators, their names conjoined on novels, articles, and essays for over a decade. Their American travels took them from New York City to Upstate New York, where they visited Sing Sing and saw the electric chair, to Niagara Falls, to Schenectady and the General Electric factory, through Poughkeepsie, Hudson, Albany, Waterloo, Sandusky, Toledo, Peoria, Springfield, Albuquerque, Flagstaff, the Sequoia National Forest. They visited Dearborn, where their trusty Ford was made, and met Henry Ford. They spent two days in Chicago, whose poverty and opulence and lawlessness terrified them. They drove past thousands of roadside billboards advertising chewing gum and Coca-Cola and Jesus, ate at drugstore luncheonettes, visited Mark Twain's boyhood home in Hannibal, Missouri, drove off the road into a ditch and were promptly rescued by a passing motorist in Texas, visited a Pueblo community in Santa Fe, passed a petrified forest and towering cacti, picked up hitchhikers, many of them in search of work, each of them with their own story, gawked at the Grand Canyon, summited the Sierra Nevadas, watched Santa Clara University and TCU play football (TCU won on a last-minute interception), and witnessed the building of the Bay Bridge. They were unimpressed by Hollywood. They were appalled by the segregation and violence of the Southern states. They were awed by American ingenuity and willingness to help others and dismayed by a culture "dominated by gangsters, and if not gangsters, then racketeers, and if not racketeers, then bankers, all of them one and the same." They worried about Germany and the possibility of war ("In five years," Mr. Adams predicted, "there will be another war"). At the General Motors factory, they worried about the effects of automation and unchecked capitalism and a culture of efficiency that valued profit over human beings.

When I first read *Roadside America*, I fell hook, line, and sinker for the call of the open road: the anticipation, the constant newness, the thrill of moving forward through space and time, the asphalt ribboning past the car window, the easy camaraderie, the companionable silences, the shared vernacular that develops when people travel thousands of miles together. My parents didn't own a car and we didn't travel much and America was so far away that it seemed like it was on another planet. I didn't know a lot, but I knew I wanted *that*.

But instead

We're in downtown Saratoga, sitting at a round wooden table in Big Basin Café. The café is nearly empty. So are our coffee cups. We've been lingering, hoping the rain would let up, but it's coming down even harder. It's been an hour since my mother and I picked up En, and we've traveled 8 miles. We're 250 miles from Solvang. There's no point in lingering further.

"We may as well, right?" I ask, and my mother and En nod in agreement, and we stand up and go.

Puddles

Submitting an application to leave the Soviet Union required receiving written permission from the parents of the applicants, even if the applicants, like my parents, were in their thirties and had their own child. And unlike Grandma Tsilya, my maternal grandparents were adamantly opposed to my parents' decision to emigrate.

My parents and I lived in an apartment in a high-rise cinder block building on the outskirts of Moscow. There was a small forest within walking distance, and one afternoon Grandma Ester and Grandpa Benya paid us a visit and the five of us–my grandparents, my parents, and I–went for a walk. The adults looked purposeful and unhappy. It had rained recently and the sky was overcast and the ground was covered with damp leaves. I walked ahead, looking for sticks and half listening to the serious voices behind me.

My mother said something I couldn't make out, then my grandfather said something else, and my mother responded, her voice raised, and then my father said something, and then my grandfather shouted, "*Vy syadete v takuy luzhu!*" I know now that *Vy syadete v takuy luzhu* is an idiomatic phrase meaning "You're going to end up in a gigantic mess," but the literal translation–and I was a literal child–is "You are going to end up sitting in such a puddle." (Later, my mother told me that my grandfather had tried to reason with her and my father, saying that at least my father had technical skills and was good with his hands. "Marcus could be a plumber or an electrician," he said, and then to my mother, "But you, what are you going to do in America? Walk the streets?")

I ran back to the grown-ups to ask what puddle my grandfather was talking about, and all four of them told me to mind my own business, and for the rest of the walk, I puzzled over why my parents–or any adults, really–would want to sit in a puddle, which everyone knew was dirty and cold and wet.

Points of origin

When I first told my husband I was writing a book about our three-day road trip, he raised his eyebrows and said, "*That's* a story?"

There are always stories that live in other stories, like the nesting dolls inside a Russian *matryoshka*. Except that the further in you go, the bigger some of the stories become, and no matter how much you try to keep them in order, they keep threatening to swallow up the story you're telling. The Greek myths were onto something: You can't escape the web of causality. Everything is related to something else. Pull one thread and another will unravel.

My husband and I met because my parents decided to leave Soviet Russia. My parents met because in June of 1941, my maternal grandparents got on the last truck out of Dzerzhinsk and because in August of 1941, my paternal grandmother got on one train out of Odesa and her sisters got on another. Agamemnon slaughtered his daughter and was slaughtered in turn because he was born into a family doomed to devour itself, over and over. Odysseus wandered for ten years and lost his entire crew because he couldn't keep his mouth shut.

The word *meander* comes from *Maiandros*, an ancient Greek name for a winding river in what is now southwestern Turkey. When someone meanders, we say they've lost the thread. Presumably, this is a reference to the story of Theseus, who vanquishes the Minotaur and then makes his way out of the labyrinth by retracing the thread he left behind as he made his way in. The thread was given to him by Ariadne, a Cretan princess who had fallen in love with him, but Ariadne's ingenuity usually receives less play than Theseus's valor. In any case, I don't think losing the thread means losing the story. Sometimes the lost thread *is* the story. A clothesline snaps in 1941, and my grandmother is left holding a baby and a useless length of rope, which becomes an anchor point.

There are many threads to this particular story. Our road trip starts in January 2023, in a downpour, with my father handing me a CB radio, but it also starts in 1941, when my father was born in Ukraine, which was then part of the Soviet Union, and in 1945, when my mother was born in Moscow, which was always part of the Soviet Union, and in 1966, when my parents met while my father was studying in Moscow and my mother was waiting outside a metro station for a girlfriend who didn't show because she caught a bad cold. It starts in 1977, when my parents and I received our exit visas and left the Soviet Union forever. It starts in New York City in 2022, when my husband and I met my second cousin, Masha, for the first time. (Why we met for the first time in 2022 is a long story; the short version is that families are complicated. Tangled, we might say.) Masha has long black hair and intense dark eyes and her favorite phrase is "I need you to understand something."

Like me, Masha came to the United States with her parents as a child; unlike me, she is a double amputee who gets around in a motorized scooter named Penelope IV. At the dinner when we first met, she casually mentioned something about the trauma that all immigrants carry and the truth of it hit me like a thunderbolt. I had always thought the trauma of immigration was for those who fled with only the clothes on their back, who rode on top of freight trains or walked hundreds of miles, who sat behind barbed wire in detention camps. My parents and I hadn't experienced that; we left on an airplane, with four suitcases, we never slept outside, we had people who helped us. We had no right to claim trauma. But trauma claimed us anyway.

Travelers, messengers, and shopkeepers

Southbound 85 runs southeast between the Santa Cruz Mountains and the Diablo Range and merges into southbound 101 near a small, inconspicuous marker commemorating the site of the first workable quicksilver mine in North America. Quicksilver is a colloquial name for mercury–a metallic element that remains liquid at room temperature and is prized for its ability to form amalgams with other metals–specifically, with silver and gold, which made it indispensable after gold was discovered in Coloma in 1848. The Roman god from whom mercury takes its name was the patron god of travelers, thieves, shopkeepers, and messengers. The ancient Greeks called him Hermes.

My mother and I have put En in charge of the music, and En is scrolling through Spotify and telling us about one of the regulars at Peet's Coffee who once gave her an envelope with a ten-dollar bill inside and who always talks about the train that used to carry stone from a quarry in the nearby hills. The train is long gone, but the tracks remain. "I mostly like everyone there, except for the guy who always asks to make sure his latte is exactly 182 degrees and the hordes of teenagers who come in when school lets out," she says. "I don't mean to be mean, but there's nothing more terrifying than a horde of teenagers, you know?"

I'm pretty sure those teenagers are students at Homestead High School, which is less than a mile away from Peet's.

"Did I ever tell you how I ended up at Homestead?" I ask.

It turns out I haven't, or if I did, En doesn't remember.

How I ended up at Homestead, a Very Good School

Before my parents and I moved to the Peninsula, we lived in a second-floor apartment on the corner of Twenty-Third Avenue and Geary Boulevard in San Francisco. Both my parents worked in Santa Clara, fifty miles away, which meant that they left for work in the early morning and returned at dinnertime, sometimes later. I was supposed to get myself to school and spend my unsupervised after-school time doing my fifth-grade homework and attending my twice-weekly gymnastics classes. I conscientiously took myself to school and conscientiously attended my gymnastics classes, but homework was a different story. Instead of doing homework, I conscientiously watched reruns of *The Brady Bunch* and *Gilligan's Island* while devouring bowl after bowl of Kellogg's Corn Pops.

The Brady Bunch and *Gilligan's Island* improved my English but complicated my relationship with my parents. My parents wanted me to study and I wanted to warm myself by the golden glow of the television, chuckling at Gilligan's antics and admiring Marcia's stick-straight blonde hair. My father unplugged the television, and I plugged it back in. My mother, fed up with the long commute and anxious about leaving me unattended from morning to night, began to talk about buying a house on the Peninsula, closer to work.

My father did not want to buy a house, either on the Peninsula or anywhere else. Shepherded by Meg, their long-suffering realtor, he and my mother looked at dozens of houses, and my father rejected every single one for implausible reasons, one more preposterous than the next.

It was only after my mother issued an ultimatum–pick a house, any house, or I take the kid and move closer to work–that he relented and agreed to make an offer on a 1960s Sunnyvale ranch house tucked in a warren of streets named after birds.

There was a lot about America my parents didn't know, but they did know this: Whatever house they bought had to be zoned for Homestead High School, not Fremont High School, because somehow, everyone knew that Homestead was a Good School and Fremont was not. The realtor assured them that the house they were about to buy was indeed zoned for Homestead High School. But two years later, when it came time to enroll me in high school, my parents discovered that the house they bought was not, in fact, zoned for Homestead.

My mother panicked and began to haunt the school district offices to see whether it would be possible to transfer me to Homestead. It was not. Rules were rules and district boundaries were district boundaries. In the Soviet Union, the way to deal with such problems would have been to slip someone an envelope or a bottle of vodka or a box of expensive chocolates, but this was America, and things didn't work that way. At last, a beleaguered attendance office clerk told my mother to bring in a note from our family doctor. "What kind of note?" asked my bewildered mother. The clerk shrugged enigmatically and said, "He'll know."

My mother cuts in and tells En that this is why I can never run for public office, and I tell her not to spoil the story.

Our family doctor was Herb Morrison, a kind and scattered man whose glasses kept sliding down his nose and whose hair was perpetually rumpled and who asked me at every single checkup until I was eighteen whether I had gotten my period yet. He also routinely confused my father and his brother Boris (who was also a patient in his practice) and asked each one to send his regards to the wrong wife. In spite of these alarming lapses, Dr. Morrison knew exactly what to do when my mother came into his office and explained our predicament. He nodded, pushed his glasses back up to the bridge of his nose, and told her he'd have a letter for her later that week.

The letter, which his receptionist handed my mother in an unsealed envelope, said that due to the trauma I experienced as a result of emigrating from the USSR and changing schools five times over six years, I was psychologically unstable. Moreover, I was (according to Dr. Morrison) so fixated on the idea that attending Homestead High School would bring much-needed stability to my life that Dr. Morrison feared I might suffer an emotional collapse were I to attend a different high school.

My mother cackles. "Psychologically unstable–can you believe it?"

As a general rule, Soviet-born people of my parents' generation don't believe in trauma. Their parents had endured pogroms, famines, mass arrests, gulags, and a war that wiped out twenty-four million people in four years, which meant that to live a reasonably predictable life with a roof over one's head and a steady source of food was to have no cause for complaint. Even the way we emigrated (by plane from Moscow to Vienna, by train from Vienna to Rome, by another plane from Rome to the United States, all with help from the Hebrew Immigrant Aid Society) was unremarkable compared to what my grandparents endured during the war years. Once we arrived in the United States, my parents found jobs, and at the time Dr. Morrison wrote his letter, we were living in a house in the heart of Silicon Valley. We had our own telephone. We had two cars in our two-car garage. We had a color television. Emotional collapse? Psychological instability? That was for weak Americans.

Nevertheless, my skeptical mother brought the letter to the district office and handed it to the clerk and the clerk put it in a file, and a week later a letter arrived at our house on Flamingo Way informing us that I was provisionally admitted to Homestead but that I would be under the supervision of a school psychologist. As soon as my condition improved, I would be sent back to Fremont. I never was.

Standing water

Crossing the Gabilan Range, with its dense groves of coastal oak, into the flats of Salinas Valley is like being inside a car wash. Gray sheets of rain obscure the farmland stretching on either side of the freeway. Gusts of wind buffet the car. Every time I change lanes–which I try to do as infrequently as possible–I can feel the meeting of rubber and water and asphalt, the wheels encountering resistance, vacillating as though they're unsure of where they want to go.

I am very sure I don't want the car to slide off the road or crash into another car, so I grip the steering wheel as hard as I can and remind myself to keep my shoulders down and to breathe and to steer into the direction of the skid if we skid and to keep the wheel steady if we hydroplane.

En has sorted out the music, and Edith Piaf's "La Vie en rose" drifts from her phone.

Il est entré dans mon coeur

My husband David and I met at Homestead High School, where I was not supposed to go. We began dating after graduation, and two months later, David went to Cornell and I went to UCLA, and with the exception of summers, when we both worked as counselors at the same summer camp, our romance was epistolary, dozens of letters traveling between Ithaca, New York, and Westwood, California. They're in a shoebox in our garage now, on a high shelf in case of flooding.

My mother and father met because my mother was also not where she was supposed to be. Or rather, she *was* supposed to be where she was: waiting for her girlfriend at a metro station, only the girlfriend got sick and didn't show. It was winter, and my mother stood in the cold and waited, and my father, who lived in Odesa at the time but happened to be studying in Moscow, saw her.

"Hold up," En bursts in. "Dedushka just came up and . . . what, like picked you up?"

"Believe it or not, yes," my mother says. "Imagine a person is waiting for someone and another person comes up to her out of nowhere and says, 'Hello.'"

This is so completely unlike my quiet, reticent father that I ask, "Just like that?"

"Just like that," says my mother.

"And then what?" I ask.

"It was freezing," she answers, "and the person says, 'Aren't you cold?' and I say, 'I'm waiting for someone,' and the person says, 'There's a café across the street. Would you like to sit somewhere warm?'"

Somewhere warm

As far back as I can remember, my parents and I spent part of each summer with my father's aunt and uncle.

Aunt Klara and Uncle Isaak lived in Odesa, but they also owned a tiny dacha in Luzanovka, a tiny beachside village on the outskirts, and that was where we stayed for weeks at a time. How Uncle Isaak managed to acquire a piece of land in a country where private ownership was prohibited is unclear, but what remains beyond dispute is that my aunt Klara was adamantly opposed to this foolish, extravagant acquisition. So was her sister-in-law, my grandma Tsilya. Every weekend, Uncle Isaak traveled from Odesa to Luzanovka, where he built a small clapboard house and planted fruit trees with help from my father and his brother Boris, and every weekend, Aunt Klara railed at him for his stupidity while Grandma Tsilya maintained that he was exploiting her boys.

Once Aunt Klara laid eyes on the finished house and the open veranda and the garden and the fruit trees, she fell in love. She cared for the fruit trees and the tomatoes and dill and green onion as tenderly as she might have cared for a baby. White, fuchsia, and pale-pink cosmos lined the whitewashed walls of the dacha. We have a black-and-white photograph of me, age six, standing in front of the cosmos, which tower over my head.

Aunt Klara and Uncle Isaak were childless, but they treated my father and my uncle as their children, which made me their de facto granddaughter, which meant I was spoiled rotten at the dacha. I did not like the apples that grew on Aunt Klara's tree and preferred the apples that grew in the neighbors' yard, and my father and Uncle Boris snuck over the fence to pick them for me when the neighbors weren't home. Aunt Klara prepared elaborate meals–fresh-caught fish, tomatoes still warm from the garden, *vareniki* (sour cherry dumplings) with sour cream–and we ate at the large table on the sun-flooded veranda. There was a lot of laughter. Fat golden apricots hung from low branches and ruby-dark sour cherries winked among the leaves. Behind the fruit trees was a green-painted outhouse everyone called "*zelenyi domik*," the little green house. In the evenings, Aunt Klara taught me to play Durak, a Russian card game. On the beach–a five-minute walk from the dacha, down a flight of splintery wooden steps–old women sold fried sunflower seeds in greasy newspaper cones.

To get to Odesa we took the overnight train, and in the evening conductors came around with strong black tea in glasses set in filigreed metal *podstakanniki*. The tea was dark amber and sloshed in concert with the rocking of the train, and one evening I saw the moon out the window. It seemed to be following us, as if by magic. I didn't tell anyone what I saw, afraid that I would break the spell, and periodically I'd peek out again, just to make sure it was there, and there it was, looking down benevolently, and I looked back, spellbound. I imagine the tea was served on the northbound train back to Moscow as well, but I can only recall the anticipatory thrill of the ride south, the magic of the moon following our train.

Family travel

Ever since En was two years old, our family spent one week of the summer at a family camp in the high Sierras. To get there from our house, we drove over Pacheco Pass, through the flat fields of California's Central Valley, and up a twisting mountain road lined with towering sequoias and pines. As we made our way up, the colors changed from dull yellows and tans to rich russets and browns and then to granite grays and stark whites. The air thinned. Our breath deepened.

There are five of us in our family: me, David, En, and her two older brothers. For many years, I described our family as dysfunctional, but that was wrong–our family *was* functioning, just not in a way that made anyone happy. Family camp was the only place we could be happy together. For six days at family camp, our fractious family became less fractious. Family camp provided three meals a day and unlimited access to four kinds of sugary cereal. It had a lake and an archery range and miles of hiking trails and trees whose tops disappeared into the sky and campfire songs and counselors in that dreamy liminal space between benzoyl peroxide and Retin-A. The counselors wore friendship bracelets and sported tattoos; they braided each other's hair and at least two or three of them played the guitar and sang beautifully. They spent the rest of the year traveling, or in college, or working odd jobs, or crashing on other people's couches. They were not tied down. They were still figuring out their lives. All of them went by their camp names–Redwood, Indigo, Strider, Sage, Achilles, Athena–and kept their real-world names secret, which added to the magic.

In college, I learned about the green world motif in Shakespeare's plays. In contrast to the unbending rules and rigid constraints of civilization and society, the green world is lush, wild, magical. The Forest of Arden, the woods in *A Midsummer Night's Dream*, the island in *The Tempest*–all places of transformation and renewal, places where characters become their authentic selves. That's what family camp was–our green world, except that when we returned home, we fell into old patterns.

When our kids were little, the first part of the drive from family camp back to Palo Alto invariably began with a discussion of what camp name each of us would choose. Fourteen years after we started going to family camp, our oldest son, a swimmer, began working there as a lifeguard and chose the name Nemo. Three years after that, his younger brother, who loves astronomy, was also hired and chose the name Orion. En is planning to work there starting in early summer of this year, and she is running through names, periodically calling out possibilities from the back seat. They include Jinx, Calico, and Jezebel. I tell her Jezebel might be a little too edgy for family camp, but she cackles and says she'll shorten it to "Jezzy."

I'm too old to work at family camp, but if I did, my camp name would be Magpie–a kind of crow with a loud, raucous call that collects objects others have discarded.

One for sorrow / Two for joy

In Western cultures, magpies are considered ill omens. They're often associated with trickery, witchcraft, misfortune. The English nursery rhyme, "One for sorrow / Two for joy / Three for a girl / Four for a boy," is rooted in ornithomancy, which goes back to the ancient Greeks, who looked to bird signs to divine the future.

A single magpie is considered bad luck because magpies are monogamous and mate for life.

We have just passed Soledad, a small town in the Salinas Valley whose name means "solitude" or "loneliness," and even though there are three of us in the car, the name feels singularly apt. Our chatter has died down and the rain has increased in intensity to the point that it feels malevolent, personal, apocalyptic. I feel utterly alone with my terror. I am responsible for getting the three of us safely to Solvang, and I don't feel remotely equal to the responsibility. It's almost impossible to see through the flooding windshield, but even if I wanted to pull over, which I don't, there's nowhere to stop. Every time I pass a truck I am absolutely certain that we will be sucked under its wheels, and even though I'm not entirely certain about how the physics of this would play out, that diminishes my terror not at all.

It's very quiet in the car except for Edith Piaf and the swishing of the wipers, which are on their highest setting, frenzied and rhythmic and inexorable, like a runaway pendulum marking off how much time we have before something terrible happens, and I think, *Out of all the bad ideas I've ever had, this is very possibly the worst.*

Going to Solvang seemed like such a good idea when my mother and I were planning the trip. A way to remember the grandmothers, now long gone, and also, who doesn't love quaint towns and little spherical pancakes? Except that now I'm pretty sure we're going to die on the way there and there will be no pancakes and it will be all my fault.

My mother is leaning forward, peering intently through the windshield–I suspect she can see even less than I can–so as to better spot oncoming danger. My father calls her cell approximately every seventeen minutes and she tells him how safe we are and how well I'm driving. Every once in a while, she asks if I want to switch, and I tell her no, I'm fine, but thank you for asking.

If you're going, go

The only way Jews could leave Soviet Russia in the 1970s was to use the burden of their Jewishness to their advantage and claim a desire to repatriate to Israel. Once out of the country, émigrés would decide on their ultimate destination–Israel for some; America, Australia, or Canada for others. The first step was to get on a plane to Vienna.

Our flight from Moscow to Vienna was full of returning Austrian tourists. There was only one family that looked like my parents and me–an anxious couple with two children, also dressed in multiple layers because not everything could fit into their allotted suitcases, also sweating profusely in the September heat–and we were too afraid to speak with each other or do anything more than make meaningful eye contact. It was obvious to the Soviet flight crew what we were: Soviet Jews who had betrayed the motherland in order to flee to the imperialist West. During the three-hour flight, I threw up into an air sickness bag, the crew treated us with withering disdain, and when we landed at Vienna International Airport and my mother hesitated before stepping off the plane, the pilot, who had emerged from the cockpit, sized her up and sneered. "*Nu chto*," he said, shrugging, "*sobralis'–idite.*" ("Well, if you're going, go.") And he gestured toward the door.

My mother told me later that it felt like she was stepping into a void. There was no coming back. We had already lost our Soviet citizenship–that happened as soon as my maternal grandparents agreed to sign our application to emigrate and my parents submitted the application to OVIR, the office in charge of visas and registrations. My parents, now considered enemies of the people, were fired from their jobs. I stayed home from third grade, which I had attended for only two weeks before our exit visas were granted. Our furniture had been sold, the apartment we lived in turned over to new residents. We had said goodbye to my grandparents, to my father's brother, to my mother's sister. That morning, I hugged my eight-year-old cousin Inna, whose weeping mother, my aunt Faina, had pushed us toward each other and said, "Who knows when you'll see each other again?" What lay ahead was entirely unknown. We didn't even know who, if anyone, would meet us at the Vienna airport.

But the pilot's sneer, the dismissive gesture toward the exit, was even worse than the unknown beyond the airplane door. My mother stiffened her spine, grabbed my hand, and marched off the plane.

Rule of threes

My parents didn't tell me that we were emigrating. After they submitted their application to leave the country, my mother was followed home by a KGB agent, and they decided that disclosing their plans to a voluble nine-year-old whose greatest ambition at the time was to be a Young Pioneer would be unwise. But I wasn't stupid: I could see that they were selling furniture, boxing up our books, packing suitcases. And one day, when I couldn't stand it anymore, I burst into our living room, where the suitcases sat open on the floor, and announced triumphantly, "I know where you're going. You're going to Israel!"

To be fair, I had no idea what or where Israel was. I had heard the name in whispered conversations where adults furtively looked around to see if anyone was listening, and it was clear to me that whatever Israel was, it was remote, dangerous, unknown, like Timbuktu or outer space. My parents exchanged startled looks, and then they stared at me in silence, and into that silence, I fired my next salvo.

"Well, no matter where you're going, I'm coming with you!" I said.

And my mother exhaled and replied, "Of course you are."

Until I left for college, it was always the three of us: the three of us on the plane from Moscow to Vienna, on the train from Vienna to Rome, on the plane from Rome to New York and from

New York to San Francisco. The three of us went on our first American road trip to Disneyland and our second American road trip to the Grand Canyon. On those trips, and just about everywhere else we went, my father was the one who drove. He drove confidently and fast. Not infrequently, he was pulled over for speeding. He taught me to drive–automatic and manual transmission–without raising his voice even once, even when I violently ground the gears on his beloved Saab. Even when I almost sideswiped another car while merging onto the freeway.

In literature, the rule of threes holds that a grouping of three–characters, obstacles, themes–is inherently more significant than any other number. There's something powerful about the number three. *Three Men in a Boat (To Say Nothing of the Dog)*, *The Three Musketeers*, *The Three Billy Goats Gruff*, the Three Bears, the Three Stooges, the Three Little Pigs, the Holy Trinity. Rock, paper, scissors. Thesis, antithesis, synthesis. Logos, ethos, pathos. Good things come in threes. So do bad things. In *Tsar Saltan*, there are three sisters, three marvels, three voyages across the sea, and thirty-three sea-knights.

Now there are three of us in the car. A troika. My mother, me, my daughter. The stylish one, the responsible one, and the fun one.

The responsible one

Among our first purchases in America was a used car—a 1973 dark blue Plymouth Satellite. My father was driving it through Park Presidio in the spring of 1978 when the right rear door flew open without warning.

My mother was in the front, imploring my father to slow down; I was in the back, mesmerized by the trees whizzing by. So much green. We'd left Moscow in September of the previous year, before the first snow, so there had been no winter as far as I could tell.

The open door made me immediately anxious. Not because I thought I was going to fall out—that didn't even occur to me—but because I was worried that in this new country, where I didn't speak the language and didn't understand how things worked, the open door was some kind of transgression. We were going to get in trouble. It was my job to prevent that from happening.

I didn't want to say anything to my parents, who were squabbling in the front seat about the advisability of speeding on a curvy road and didn't notice the open door. "The road is not curvy," my father said. My mother retorted that it absolutely was curvy and asked him whether he wanted to end up in an *avariya*, a car accident. I didn't want to interrupt, so I began inching toward the gap between the body of the car and the open door on my stomach. No seat belt, because it was 1978 and I was in the back seat and everyone knew the back seat was the safest place in the car. The blue vinyl bench seat in the back was slippery, but not too slippery, thanks to the stitching that scored the vinyl from top to bottom every inch or so.

I understood the physics intuitively: keep as much of my body as I can inside the car and use my arms to grab the open door and pull it toward me. I would be a *plastun*, a member of the Cossack infantry, whose name comes from the word *plast*–flat and low. Because the door was too far away for me to remain entirely in the car, I stretched my arms as far as I could, my head following, and I could see the asphalt whipping by below me. My mother was right: My father was going too fast. For a brief moment, it occurred to me that I could fall out of the car, probably flat on my face, and then my parents would have yet another thing to worry about, but then my fingertips grazed the bottom of the door and I pulled as hard as I could. The door resisted–the Plymouth Satellite was a substantial American car, and the substantial American wind added to the resistance–but I pulled it close enough to grab the handle and slam the door shut with a satisfying thud.

My parents stopped squabbling and looked back, startled. "What happened?" my mother asked.

"Nothing," I said.

The fun one

In the back seat, En pops open her energy drink and asks my mother if she wants to try a Monster.

My mother gives her a perplexed look. "A monster?"

"Yeah," En says, "it's an energy drink. It's fizzy."

I ask En if she was trying to poison my mother, who as a matter of general policy avoids anything chemically processed, artificially sweetened, or mass-produced. I'm also biased, because I hate carbonated beverages. "Did you know," I ask, "that carbonation triggers the same pain receptors in the nasal cavity as mustard and horseradish but most of the population is insensitive to that particular pain?"

"Did you know," En replies, "that you're a weirdo? And you're making that up."

"I am not a weirdo. I'm a delicate flower," I say. "And I am not making that up. I read it in an article somewhere."

To everyone's surprise, my mother takes a swig and pauses judiciously before swallowing and pronouncing it delicious.

En cackles–*heh heh heh*, but more nasal, a high, twanging, witchy cackle that startles me and sends my mother into a paroxysm of laughter.

"Are you a witch?" she asks En.

"Nah, I'm just practicing my new laugh," En says. "What do you think?" (Later, En will tell me that the laugh was meant to break up the sense of silent dread in the car. It will become a running joke during our trip: My mother will try to replicate En's cackle, fail, and request that En do it. En will oblige, happily.)

"You sound like Baba Yaga," my mother says.

In Russian folklore, Baba Yaga is a witch who lives in the forest and feasts on lost travelers and small children. She lives in a hut made of human bones that perambulates on chicken legs at her bidding, although for travel that requires covering long distances at high velocity, she flies in a mortar and pestle.

"Baba Yaga is a badass," En says.

Modes of transportation

We did not have a car in the Soviet Union. No one we knew did. My parents and I took buses and streetcars and trains, and, on very rare occasions, a taxi. Until we arrived in San Francisco, my mother had never been behind the wheel of a car.

My father, who got his driver's license within two weeks of our arrival, taught her how to drive. The driving lessons were fraught, and by fraught I mean that my mother gripped the wheel like her life depended on it and my father sat in the passenger seat, coiled like a cobra in anticipation of her next mistake. I sat in the back, monitoring the front seat for signs of trouble.

Trouble arrived hard and fast, usually in the first five minutes of our excursion. My father would explode when my mother forgot to look over her shoulder before changing lanes, or spent too long looking over her shoulder, or rested her foot in the wrong place. It seemed that her foot was always resting in the wrong place. "Where are you resting your foot?" he would yell, and then I'd yell, "Stop yelling at Mom!" and he would yell at me to stop yelling and my mother would yell at him for yelling at me.

My mother was not a confident driver. She failed her driving exam twice. She almost failed on her third attempt, but it was New Year's Eve, and the examiner looked at her white knuckles on the steering wheel, her imploring eyes, and circled "pass."

Getting her driver's license did not make my mother more confident. Shortly after passing the behind-the-wheel exam, she was driving to a supermarket on Geary Boulevard in a downpour and couldn't find the lever that activated the windshield wipers. The cars behind us were honking because she was barely inching along and I tried to explain to her where the lever was because I had been paying attention during the practice driving sessions, but she was panicking and fumbling so I took off my seat belt and crawled across her lap and pulled the right lever. "Irisha, you're brilliant," she said, exhaling gratefully.

My American name

I was born Irina Markusovna–Irina, daughter of Markus. The name Irina comes from the ancient Greek *eirene*, which means peace. Markus comes from Mars, the Roman god of war. I'm pretty sure Grandma Tsilya was not familiar with the Roman pantheon when she named my father, and I'm equally sure my parents were not aware of my name's Greek origins when they named me. Irina is a common Russian name–the Russian equivalent of the American Jennifer or Emily.

My Russian name, Irina, comes with multiple diminutives–Irochka, Ira, Irisha. My mother calls me Irisha. My father calls me Irochka.

When we came to the United States, my father decreed that my American name would be Irene. I was outraged to my core by this arbitrary renaming; I spoke no English, but Irene was a name that struck me as alien and sterile, and I didn't care if Irina was not an American name. My father said, "It's just easier" when I protested. Then he left the room and I went over to the kitchen table where he had been filling out our green card applications and saw that while it would be difficult to change the middle *e* to an *i*, it would be easy to change the terminal *e* to an *a* with a single downward stroke, which is what I did. When he saw what I had done, he half smiled, half shrugged, and that was how I became Irena, with an *a* at the end.

The stylish one

My mother is small and elegant. She wears her auburn hair in a short, sharp-edged bob, favors structured jackets with kimono sleeves, and has been compared, not inaccurately, to Edna Mode in *The Incredibles.*

In Soviet Russia, where studying art or literature was prohibited to Jews, she became a chemistry teacher, and now, after decades spent working as an engineer, she works as a museum docent. She sweeps through the echoing galleries with a regal confidence, like it's her birthright. She is irresistibly drawn to beauty, and she has spent decades lamenting my disgraceful behavior during our visit to St. Petersburg when I was seven, because I spent the entire time looking through a kaleidoscope instead of at the priceless art in the Hermitage Museum.

It's been over forty years, and my mother still can't let it go. She tells En about my juvenile philistinism, and En chortles with delight. I point out that when we visited the Hermitage in 1975, my mother and father already knew that we would leave the Soviet Union forever, but no one told me, a small child, and also, they bought me a kaleidoscope that very morning, and what did they think would be more interesting to a small child–a new kaleidoscope or fine art? Of course my parents' enthusiastic entreaties–"Look, Irisha! Just look!"–fell on deaf ears as we walked mile after mile down opulent hallways, past Caravaggio's

The Lute Player, Rembrandt's *The Return of the Prodigal Son*, Titian's *Danaë*, Gauguin's *Woman Holding a Fruit*. Decades later, I have vague memories of gilded opulence, buxom naked women, bowls of fruit, boredom, aching feet. I remember the kaleidoscope much more clearly, the piercing wonder of the patterns unfurling, contracting, changing color and shape, an entire universe at the end of a tube.

"Do you know," my mother says, suddenly serious, "I sometimes dream of being back at the Hermitage. I'm walking through the galleries, and no one is there, and I'm just walking alone, for hours, looking at all the art."

Arts and crafts

When I was ten or eleven, Grandma Tsilya tried to teach me to sew. Her stitches were even and straight. Mine were crooked. She shook her head and sighed. "*Leymene en hant*," she muttered. Hands of clay.

When I was in college, she despaired over my friendship bracelets. She called them *tryapochki*, little rags, their fraying ends an affront. She couldn't countenance unfinished seams, puckered hemlines, loose threads.

Before she was Grandma Tsilya, she was simply Tsilya, or Tsilechka, the youngest in a family of five that lived in a small Ukrainian settlement called Lyubashovka. Her parents owned a fabric store, but it was her mother who ran it while her father pored over Torah scrolls. My great-grandmother traveled to buy fabric, probably to Odesa, a port city. I'm imagining her peering at slippery satins, diaphanous chiffons, heavy gabardines, delicate batistes, bright flower-sprigged chintzes, examining the drape, considering the hand. I imagine a sumptuous dark blue-green fabric among them, the color of a cresting wave.

My great-grandmother was careful to keep sharp objects out of the hands of the baby, but at age three–or so the story goes–little Tsilya found a needle and thread and some fabric scraps and made a dress for her doll. From then on, she was given unfettered access to sewing supplies. I imagine her clutching those scraps, that doll, when she and her parents and older sisters hid in the neighbors' cellar during pogroms that swept through Lyubashovka and left ransacked shops and smoldering ruins and bodies maimed or torn or burned beyond recognition. After her husband died, she supported herself and her two sons–my father and my uncle Boris–by taking in sewing, which had to be done on the sly, with the curtains drawn, because engaging in private enterprise could land you in prison. She could sew anything–suits, jackets, special-occasion dresses, everyday dresses, children's clothing. She knitted sweaters and scarves. When my mother was pregnant with me and there was no maternity wear to be had anywhere, she sewed maternity dresses that were so strikingly stylish that my mother swears they inspired several of her coworkers to get pregnant.

In Russian, the word *kroit'* means to cut (specifically in the context of sewing), but it also means to put together parts of a pattern, to use sheets of paper to create pieces of fabric that, when joined at the edges, become a three-dimensional article of clothing. It's a double-edged word, a contronym like *cleave*, which means both to join together and to cut asunder. The verb *kroit'* is related to the noun *krai*–the generic name for the territories on the edges of the Russian Empire. *Krai* lurks in the name *Ukraina* and in the word *okraina,* which refers to land that lies on the periphery.

The hero of this book

Grandma Ester and Grandpa Benya lived in central Moscow, a forty-minute metro ride from our cinder block apartment building on the outskirts. On one of our visits, I was sliding a ceramic cat on their living room rug and quietly narrating the cat's movements when I heard my mother and my grandfather talking about me in the kitchen. "She's not especially pretty, but there's an *izyuminka* to her," my grandfather said, and my mother agreed.

Izyuminka is a Russian diminutive for *izyum*, raisin, and it made absolutely zero sense to me that a person would have a raisin in them, even a little one, so on the way home, I asked my mother what she and my grandfather were talking about. She scolded me for eavesdropping and then explained that an *izyuminka* was not an actual raisin. It was more like a spark, or a bit of spice. "He meant that you're not dull," she said. "What about pretty?" I asked. My mother said, "Don't be vain."

But I am vain. I want to be the hero of this story. I want to be the hero of my own life. If the *Odyssey* is a poem about *nostos*, a longing to return to hearth and home, and the *Iliad* is a poem about *kleos*, glory and acclaim won in battle, I want both. In the underworld, the ghost of Achilles tells Odysseus that he would rather be a lowly farmer tilling the earth than king of all the breathless dead, but I don't buy it. Who wouldn't want to be king? As a child, I used to eavesdrop on my mother's telephone conversations to see if she would say something nice about me. I want acclaim. I want glory. I want to be seen.

What the Greeks Knew

In college, I studied English, and then, because I wasn't sure what to do after graduation, I went to graduate school for comparative literature. My dissertation was about physical and semantic displacement in the novels of Henry James and Vladimir Nabokov—the former an American expatriate who chose to live in England, the latter a Russian refugee who arrived in America by way of England, Germany, and France, fleeing first the Russian Revolution and then the Second World War. Both putatively American authors who were not entirely, or exactly, American.

Why did I choose James and Nabokov? Why does anyone do anything? Because I had to. Because it was fated. Because I saw myself in them—their lack of full belonging to this country or that, in their deliberate, artful distancing from the degradations and uncertainties of exile. Because I aspired to Nabokov's sinuous prose—"I was a perfectly normal trilingual child in a family with a large library," he once remarked casually—and because of James's preoccupation with money and status, which fascinated me because for many years my family had neither. James created characters who left America and traveled to Europe and Nabokov created characters who fled Europe and traveled to America, and their characters suffered because they were too worldly and refined in a country full of cheerful, materialistic imbeciles or they were very rich and very naive and surrounded by sophisticated, calculating schemers. But mostly, I chose them because I wanted to believe–and don't we all want to believe this?–that I was the master of my fate and the captain of my soul. Invincible, unbowed. I was not like James's naive Americans abroad and I was not like Nabokov's damaged exiles in America. I was neither overly trusting nor stubbornly hidebound; I had risen above being no one and belonging nowhere; I could see the big picture. I had transcended the indignities of being an immigrant, gloriously; I could maneuver seamlessly between and within cultures and languages. My dissertation was proof of that.

The ancient Greeks knew about fate. They knew about reversals of fortune–how suddenly a road can swerve into an abyss, how delicious it is to watch others brought low. Isn't that why we read books and watch plays and films and TV shows about bad things that happen to other people?

Speaking of which

About a hundred miles into our drive, after my animal terror about getting us all killed fades into resigned wariness, I introduce the second season of *The White Lotus* into our conversation. We haven't crashed yet. Maybe we won't. And even if we do, at the very least I can let my mother and En know about my latest enthusiasm.

I have a tendency to become obsessed with television shows. I can still quote long stretches of dialogue from *The Brady Bunch* and *Gilligan's Island.* I know every single one of Alexis's last names on *Dynasty*, which my mother and I watched religiously every Wednesday night: Alexis Morell Carrington Colby Dexter. I evangelize about the in-your-face crassness of *Married with Children* ("That's what happens when you only gain four pounds during your pregnancy," Al Bundy says to his wife, gesturing at their dim-witted daughter) and about the masterful narrative arc of *Mad Men* and *Bad Sisters.* I can't help myself. A good story well told is irresistible.

I hadn't meant to watch the second season of *The White Lotus.* But all through December, my social media was buzzing with impassioned discussions of Portia's wardrobe ("Portia vs. the aesthetics of beauty") and enticingly cryptic exhortations ("Send me to the White Lotus. I need a vacation and I want to die") and images juxtaposing Peppa Pig and Jennifer Coolidge swathed in exuberantly flowered pink chiffon. I wanted to participate in the discourse, so I started watching, and once I started, I couldn't stop.

Now, in the car, I can't stop talking about it. I finished the season a few days before our trip, and the show is still churning in my head–the restless sea, the sumptuous lodgings, the arrogance, the gullibility, the scheming, the elegant unfurling of the plot. I try to explain how it reminds me of Henry James–wealthy, oblivious Americans in Europe–but with a dark undercurrent of something ancient and primal and malevolent. But also funny. Maybe we can watch the first episode in Solvang, I suggest, then think, *Assuming we don't die en route*, because it's never a good idea to drop one's guard.

En is unenthusiastic. I can see her grimace in the rearview mirror; she says she's seen the first few episodes of the first season and doesn't understand what the fuss is about. "Blah blah blah, terrible rich people, blah blah blah, Hawaii, blah blah, stupid girls taking ketamine" is how she sums up season one, then adds that if season two is like that, she is definitely not interested. My mother has no idea what *The White Lotus* even is. "Like the flower?" she wants to know.

The lotus flower

In Book IX of the *Odyssey*, Odysseus and his men are blown off course by storm winds and end up in the land of the lotus-eaters, whose inhabitants subsist on a plant that makes all those who eat it forget their home and those they love. After tasting the plant, Odysseus's men loll about in a placid torpor, and it is only with great effort that Odysseus manages to rouse them and return them to the ships. By "great effort," I mean that he dragged them back and chained them to the rowing benches.

The ancient Greek historian Herodotus was convinced that the lotus-eaters still existed somewhere in coastal Libya; some three hundred years later, Polybius placed them on the island of Djerba, off the coast of Tunisia. Some historians speculate that the lotus flower was not a lotus at all, but a poppy with narcotic properties. It's also possible that it was a fruit of the date-palm tree or a blue lotus, which was well-known in ancient Egypt and used for its soporific and psychotropic properties.

What I want to know is this: Is it fair to call someone a hero when they begin their relatively straightforward journey home with twelve ships, take ten years to reach their destination, and lose every single ship and every single one of their men along the way?

But not that kind

The premise of *The White Lotus*, I explain, is that there's a dead body in the opening episode, but we don't know whose, or why, or how. The remainder of the show is devoted to retracing what happens from the time the central characters arrive to the discovery of the dead body. In season 2, the central characters include two married couples vacationing together; a wealthy, recently married heiress and her personal assistant; and three generations of men who have come to Sicily to explore their roots. There are also two local girls who are–I dither over the nomenclature–hookers. Or, no, sex workers. Or prostitutes?

"Mom," En says, exhaling loudly, and sticks her head between our two seats. "No one says 'sex worker' anymore. You can't really dress up that people are being exploited. It's okay to say prostitute or hooker."

Edith Piaf warbles that she regrets nothing, neither the good nor the evil that was done to her.

But that's the thing, I say. It's complicated, the exploitation, like who is exploiting whom? ("Whomst," En corrects me from the back seat, and chuckles.) And also, the scenery! The clothes! The acting! The writing! Seriously, I tell them, it's like nothing I'd ever seen.

Because I have a tendency toward hyperbole, both En and my mother look skeptical. I don't actually see them look skeptical because I'm focusing on the road, but I can feel their skepticism and wonder if, in the same way, they can feel my fear that I will kill us all.

Chimera

By the time we stop in Buellton for a late lunch, the rain has slowed to a drizzle.

I can pinpoint when the rain started letting up: somewhere around Templeton, where I saw a sign reading LOS OSOS and asked En to look up whether *oso* means bear in Spanish. En exhaled dramatically and said, "OMG, *why* do you need to know?" in an aggrieved voice and I told her I was curious because *oso* sounded like *ursa*, Latin for bear, and she said I could look it up myself later and I told her I had been driving for three hours in terrible conditions and looking up a single solitary word was the least she could do to support me, and then my mother said, "Speaking of terrible weather, it looks like the rain is letting up a little."

My mother is right: After Templeton, the drive feels far less dire. The relentless downpour relents, the road curves through thickly wooded hills, and then the hills part and we catch a glimpse of the Pacific Ocean, cloud-choked and gray, enormous waves breaking on the shore. Then the road turns inland again, winding through a startlingly green forest. I reduce the wiper speed to medium.

And then we're in Buellton, population 5,106, famous for Pea Soup Andersen's–an old-timey restaurant founded in 1924 that boasts serving two million bowls of pea soup a year. None of us wants pea soup, so we opt for Industrial Eats, an eatery in a barnlike building where diners sit at long communal tables and eat pizza and salads made from locally sourced ingredients.

Easing the car into a parking space feels like falling into bed at the end of a long day. I pull back my shoulders and flex my fingers, which ache with the effort of gripping the steering wheel for five hours. My shoulders ache too. My neck twangs when I turn my head. My eyes hurt. I'm exhausted and slightly delirious and proud of myself for not killing anyone and also, suddenly, ravenous. We go inside and order several pizzas, which have blistered thin crusts and toppings like fennel sausage and pasilla chile and taleggio cheese and chard, and find a long unoccupied wooden table in a back room next to a giant woodburning fireplace. I take a selfie of the three of us but we're all looking in different directions, none of them at the camera, and my mother and I look far older and more tired than I would like to think we look in real life.

When we emerge, flushed and dazed with warmth and food, it's nearly dark. A fine mist hangs in the air. We're only eight miles from Solvang–a laughably easy drive–when we pass a fenced field with indistinct black shapes that look vaguely bovine but are far too tall to be cows. "Are those cows?" I ask. "Are they standing on their hind legs? What is happening?"

En squints through the mist and agrees that they're definitely weird looking. Then she spots a sign.

The sign reads OSTRICHLAND USA. Nearby is a billboard depicting a painted life-sized ostrich with the caption FEED THIS BAD BOY!

En claps her hands and says, "Oh my god, ostriches! We have to go to the ostrich farm. We *have* to. Please?"

Antipodes

The ostriches remind En of Australia. In her senior year of high school, she found an experiential learning program in the South Pacific–a month in Fiji, where students lived with host families and learned about tribal hierarchies and helped prepare breadfruit and cassava; a month in New Zealand studying Indigenous culture and marine biology; and a month in Australia, where En and two other girls came across a cassowary on a hike. Cassowaries, says En, are related to ostriches, but far scarier.

The one she encountered looked like a riled-up dinosaur–large, menacing, murderous. "You don't understand–they have this crazy coloring, and this weird thing on their heads, and claws that can totally rip you open. See?" she says, holding her phone up to my mother. My mother asks if that's a picture from the Internet and En tells her no, she took the photo as the cassowary began advancing on them.

"A murderous bird is walking toward you and you take a picture?" I ask. "Seriously? I would have run."

En says that she was planning on it–was backing away, in fact–but Ellie, a girl in her group, stayed put and started speaking to the bird. She called it "hanischka," which apparently was a term of endearment based on a diminutive of "honey" in Ellie's family. Eventually, En and the other girl persuaded Ellie to back away. En reports that Ellie sang out, "Bye, hanischka, bye!" as the cassowary disappeared into the forest.

"Like it was her best friend!" En says.

I find the phrase "Bye, hanischka, bye!" hilarious and repeat it several times until my mother opines that Ellie is an idiot. Who would willingly approach a bird the size of a human being with daggers for feet, she wants to know.

"Okay, but Babushka, we *must* see the ostriches," En says again. "I'm sure they're in a cage or something."

She looks up Ostrichland USA on her phone and announces that they open at 10 a.m. the following morning, and since our only firm plans at this point involve being in Paso Robles in time to see the light installation, my mother and I agree to see the ostriches.

"Even though I thought they were cows standing on their hind legs, and you know how I feel about cows," I say.

Tree. Field. Shouting.

I hate cows with a vengeance and without exception.

When I was four, my maternal grandparents rented a dacha outside of Moscow for the summer. My grandfather and I went for a walk, through a field and then down a narrow path through the woods, where I picked flowers called Ivan-da-Marya, which are half purple and half yellow. In Russian, *Ivan da Marya* means Ivan and Marya, although I could never figure out which one–Ivan or Marya–was supposed to be purple and which yellow. In English, the flowers are called wood cow-wheat. My grandfather pointed out several red-capped mushrooms; they were called *mukhomor*, a sinister-sounding name that yokes together the word *mukha* (fly) and *mor* (death). "Never touch one," he said. "Don't even get close. They kill almost instantly," and I peered at the red-capped mushrooms cautiously, astonished that something so small could be so lethal.

We retraced our steps to return to the dacha, and as we were cutting through the field, I heard shouting far away, and then closer, and some kind of commotion I didn't understand, and suddenly my grandfather picked me up and ran to a tree and lifted me high into the branches, and it was only then that I realized there was a bull charging across the field, straight for us, and the shepherd was chasing the bull and shouting, and my grandfather was also shouting, and I understood that he had put me in a tree so that the bull wouldn't kill me when it reached us but that it would almost certainly kill my grandfather.

He's going to get knocked down and trampled, I thought, and at the same time, *And I'll have no way to get down. I'll be stuck in this tree forever.* Even amid the shouting and the terror, I recognized how selfish the second thought was as soon as it popped into my head. But it was too late to unthink it.

The shepherd managed to distract the bull before it reached my grandfather and my grandfather yelled something angry-sounding at the shepherd, and the shepherd shouted something equally angry-sounding back, and then my grandfather lifted me out of the tree and we walked back to the dacha. I kept turning around to make sure we were safe.

A brief digression

You know who else turns around? Lot's wife in the Book of Genesis. Orpheus in Hades, right before he and Eurydice reach daylight. Look what happens to them: Lot's wife turns into a pillar of salt. Orpheus's beloved wife vanishes into thin air. The message seems to be just keep going. *Sobralis'–idite.* Or, as Dory says in *Finding Nemo,* just keep swimming.

Accommodations

It's already dark when we arrive at Wine Valley Inn & Cottages.

My mother reserved two rooms in the main building–one for her, one for me and En. When we discussed travel logistics, she announced she was going to get her own room, which took me aback because I envisioned a cozy sleepover-type situation, her in one bed, me and En in another. When I asked her what was wrong with sharing a room, she snippily told me that she wanted her own space and her own bathroom.

My mother grew up in a communal apartment, with a family in each bedroom and one kitchen and one bathroom for nineteen people, so this made sense. I still didn't like it, but I understood where she was coming from. When she and her younger sister Faina were little, they almost died because one of the neighbors was boiling laundry on the stove and the soap got into the porridge my grandmother was making for them. The neighbor with the laundry admitted to this only after both girls became violently ill and Grandma Ester began interrogating all the neighbors and wouldn't stop.

En and I are not like that. We would never leave laundry boiling on the stove. But–and it pains me to admit this–we are not *not* like that. Except that I've learned to be socially acceptable about my messiness and En has not. I'm like Carmy's kitchen in

The Bear–controlled chaos and repressed anguish–and she's like Jobu's Everything Bagel in *Everything Everywhere All at Once*.

En does not believe in pillboxes, because they're "for old people," and instead travels with five containers of prescription medication that she sometimes remembers to take and other times does not. She tends to spread her possessions out in concentric circles but not in any kind of intentional way. This is because she's thinking about a million things at once and because the idea of folding and organizing and arranging is exhausting and overwhelming. I can usually hold myself together, but in close proximity to En's kind of chaos, I start to unravel.

My mother finishes unpacking and arranging her jars of potions and creams and vitamins in her room across the hall and comes into our room to see if we're ready to explore Solvang by night.

We are not. I'm on my computer answering work emails and En is digging in her duffel bag and flinging away irrelevant items because she can't find her pants. She took her jeans off when we came into our room and now she can't find those either, nor can she find her *other* pants, which she's positive she has packed.

My mother looks darkly and disapprovingly around our room and hisses, in Russian, "Why do you put up with this?"

Before I can answer, she adds, "She's twenty-two years old," and gives me a meaningful look. I say nothing, and she continues, "How can anyone live like this?"

Yep, not ideal, but she's living, I think but do not say.

En is still rifling through her bag, but her shoulders tighten visibly, because while my mother's Russian might have been incomprehensible to her, the intonation is not.

I shut my laptop and say, "Babushka and I are just going across the hall to her room." I add that we'll probably walk downtown in ten minutes or so and En can join us later if she wants.

Then I muscle my mother into her tidy room and shut the door.

How could you

"How can you put up with this?" my mother demands even before the door clicks shut.

When I was in high school, tiny, fierce Grandma Tsilya, who often took issue with how I was dressed, routinely waylaid my mother at family gatherings, backed her against a wall, and hissed, "How could you let her go out dressed like that?"

How did I dress when I was in high school? I wore my father's old *telnyashka*, a black-and-white striped undershirt, and long skirts, and leg warmers (even though I was not a dancer), and a thrifted, threadbare denim jacket, and too much black eyeliner. I wanted to look bohemian and *artsy*. I could already feel the stirrings of a restlessness that told me I did not belong here, in Sunnyvale. Where I belonged, I wasn't sure, but I wanted to go *somewhere*–New York, maybe, or Paris. I would sit in a café with a cigarette, dressed in a long skirt and vintage cardigan, sipping espresso and . . . writing, probably? My imagination stopped there, but I was preparing: amassing a mostly black wardrobe, refusing to use capital letters, cultivating a world-weary demeanor. My wardrobe was far from scandalous, but Grandma Tsilya objected nonetheless. It was sloppy. It was inappropriate.

My flustered mother took Grandma Tsilya's indignation out on me when we returned home, even though she herself had no specific objections to how I dressed. Later, when I was in graduate school, Grandma Tsilya stopped using my mother as an intermediary and began criticizing me directly. She gestured despairingly at my flowing skirts and Doc Martens and asked whether this was how I dressed for work. At the time, I was a teaching assistant in intro-level humanities and composition courses at UCLA, and how I dressed was considered fancy by my generally disheveled cohort, but Grandma Tsilya would be satisfied with nothing less than pantyhose and pumps and a prim, well-tailored skirt and blouse. But by then, her pressing urgency had given way to a grudging surrender to my inscrutable American ways, and anyway, I was married, and it no longer mattered how I dressed.

The door clicks shut and I give my mother a leveling look.

"En has ADHD," I say. "She's messy and disorganized. Feel free to be outraged, but asking me how she can live like this isn't going to fix anything." I pause, and then, because I can't not say it, I add, "And she's living–maybe not in a way you like, but she's alive, and if there's anything I've learned over the past four years, it's that interacting with people based on who you want them to be and how you want them to act is . . . not helpful."

My mother looks stricken. Her outrage wilts.

"So then . . . what? Do we just let her live like a pig in a sty?" Resigned, no longer angry.

"Pretty much," I say. "We're going to be together for two more days. We can choose to fight the whole time, or we can choose to enjoy our time together."

My mother starts to answer, but at that moment En knocks on the door and sings out, "I'm ready!"

All this way and for what

Under different circumstances–had it been sunny, had the three of us not been out of sorts after the long drive and the kerfuffle at the hotel–we might have found Solvang's half-timbered houses and thatched roofs and windmills charming. But even though it's early evening, many of its shops and restaurants are shuttered post-Christmas or pre-storm or both, and Solvang seems at once gaudy and inhospitable, like a stage set abruptly abandoned by the cast. Water drips from the eaves. We keep weaving to avoid puddles on the sidewalk and bumping into each other. We don't feel like dinner because of our late lunch, but we want *something*, so we wander aimlessly around the downtown until we find an open bakery. It's packed with tourists and prepackaged cookies. The pastries we order are fine but not extraordinary and the coffee comes in Styrofoam cups and the only available creamer is half-and-half in little plastic containers, and as we sit there complaining about the coffee and the creamer and the so-so pastries, I think how ridiculous we must look, three women who just survived a hair-raising drive through a violent storm fussing about mediocre coffee and the absence of almond milk.

Which is how we end up watching the first episode of *The White Lotus*. There's nothing else to do in nighttime Solvang, so we return to the hotel and climb onto my mother's king-sized bed. My mother sits to my left; En sits to my right. I sit in the middle, the laptop in my lap, and press "play."

Siren song

Among the many dangers Odysseus encounters as he makes his way back to Ithaca are the Sirens–half-bird, half-human creatures whose enchanting song lures sailors to their doom. As his ship nears the rocky, bone-strewn-island where the Sirens dwell, Odysseus instructs his men to stop their ears with wax and to tie him to the mast so that he alone might hear the Sirens' song and live. The song is so bewitching that Odysseus nearly loses his mind; only the rope binding him to the mast and the unhearing, dogged rowing of his crew saves him and the other men from certain death.

The theme music of *The White Lotus* is insistent and urgent and insidious and beguiling. Subdued piano chords at first, then an ethereal, ululating human voice without words, a quickening synthesizer beat, mandolin, piano again. Accompanying the fevered, throbbing music is a cascade of fevered, throbbing images, a lewd fresco come to life. A chained monkey, a swan astride a woman, a couple riding an ass, a goat mounting another goat, a spurting fountain, a dagger, a man sucking on a woman's breast, a man sucking on another man.

I was so enraptured with the idea of *The White Lotus* that I never stopped to consider the reality of *The White Lotus*–the quasi-pornographic opening sequence and everything that follows. Was it advisable–was it appropriate–to watch this show with my mother on one side of me and my daughter on the other? Probably not, but it's too late. We're at a turning point. Both of them are already leaning forward, entranced.

Turning point

At the Vienna airport, my parents and I were met almost immediately by two representatives of Sokhnut, an agency that helped repatriate Soviet Jews to Israel. Had my parents indicated that they wished to proceed to Israel, we would have been on the next plane to Tel Aviv. But my parents wished to proceed to the United States, so the Sokhnut representatives looked at us scornfully and left, and that was that–one road not taken, the other unclear. We waited forlornly next to our suitcases for several hours before a harried-looking woman found us and shepherded us through the airport to a large black car.

She drove us to a residential hotel filled with other recently arrived Soviet Jews waiting to be processed by the US-based Hebrew Immigrant Aid Society. Once the processing was complete, we would proceed to Rome to wait for our request for political asylum to be approved or denied by the United States.

I sat quietly in the back of the car next to my mother while the adults made halting small talk in a combination of German and Russian, my mother thumbing feverishly through a Russian–German dictionary. When we climbed out in front of the hotel, my father whispered, "Mercedes!" to my mother, and even though I had no idea what a Mercedes was, I could tell by his voice that it was a good thing.

The pleasures of schadenfreude

There is something deeply satisfying in watching rich people having a terrible time in one of the most beautiful places on earth.

The English word *vacation* comes from the Latin *vacatio*, which means free, unoccupied, released from service. The Russian word for vacation, *otpusk*, comes from the verb *otpustit'*, to let something or someone go. To go on vacation is to be set free, to be transported to a world beyond daily drudgery.

And yet everyone at the White Lotus seems dissatisfied. A young woman with questionable taste in clothes is at the mercy of the needy, capricious heiress for whom she works as a personal assistant. The heiress, who favors billowing dresses and extravagantly impractical stiletto-heeled sandals, is worried that her husband is having an affair. The heiress's husband is irritated, both with his flamboyant wife and with the fact that his wife brought her personal assistant on what was supposed to be a romantic vacation for two. An attorney frets that she and her husband, who just sold his company and made a fortune, are LARPing as rich people. They're vacationing with the husband's college roommate, a smugly arrogant finance bro, and his sunny, vacuous, fetching wife, and they have adjoining rooms but nothing in common. Three generations of men—a grandfather, his son, and his grandson—are in Italy to track down their family roots; the grandfather is a flatulent lecher, the father is a serial adulterer whose wife has had it with the endless cheating, and the grandson is a fresh-faced college graduate trying to navigate between the two older men and his mother, who has chosen to remain home in Los Angeles and possibly initiate divorce proceedings. Valentina, the hotel manager, is exasperated by the incompetence of her staff, the ridiculous demands of the entitled guests, and her unacknowledged crush on Isabella, a young, earnest hotel employee.

The only people who seem to be free of care are Lucia and Mia–the local girls in short dresses who walk down to the pier and watch as the boat carrying the guests arrives at the resort. Lucia has arranged to meet one of the new guests for sex, but she doesn't yet know who it is. Mia is tagging along because Lucia is her best friend. Their banter is uncomplicated, easy, full of laughter. Lucia is sucking on a giant rainbow swirl lollipop like a child without a care in the world.

La dolce vita

In early October of that year, after our paperwork was processed, we left Vienna for Rome on a train full of Soviet émigrés. At the Roma Termini, our train was met by young men in white shirts, gold chains glinting on their chests, large guns slung across their chests. When I asked my mother who they were, she shushed me. Much later, I would learn that they were mafiosi who had been hired by the Hebrew Immigrant Aid Society as a deterrent against terrorist attacks. It had never occurred to me before then that we were important enough to be destroyed.

Aebleskiver

I wake up to the sun shining through our room window and En scrolling on her phone for places to eat breakfast–specifically, the little spherical pancakes that had so enchanted both my grandmothers many years ago. After consulting Yelp (founded in Silicon Valley in 2004 by two former employees of Palo Alto–based PayPal), she announces that we should have breakfast at the Solvang Restaurant, a five-minute walk from our hotel, and we navigate to the restaurant using Google Maps (Google: founded in Palo Alto in 1998 by two Stanford graduate students, one of whom left Moscow with his parents two years after I left Moscow with mine). The Solvang Restaurant boasts a wooden sign with ornate Gothic lettering, murals depicting scenes from Hans Christian Andersen fairy tales, and world-famous aebleskiver.

We drink coffee (again without plant-based milk) and eat aebleskiver (which are, indeed, delicious) and plot our next move. En reminds us several times that we have to see the ostriches, and since we're in no particular hurry, my mother and I agree that Ostrichland USA will be our first stop after checking out of the hotel. After that, we'll make a stop at Bob's Well Bread in the town of Los Olivos on the recommendation of a friend who lives in Ventura. "But we just had breakfast," my mother objects. "Second breakfast," En and I say in unison.

My mother does not know about second breakfast, so En and I give her a quick tutorial on hobbits and their eating habits, and my mother is compelled to acknowledge that a second breakfast does not sound like a terrible thing. "Also, we're on an adventure," I point out, feeling far bolder than I did yesterday, when all I wanted was for the three of us not to die. "We need to fortify ourselves. And Los Olivos is sort of on the way to Paso Robles, plus we don't need to be at the light installation until 4:30 at the earliest."

"Unrelated," En cuts in, "but I think Ethan in *White Lotus* kills someone. He's got this blank thousand-yard stare, don't you think? And this really expressionless face, like a sociopath."

Because I know things En and my mother do not yet know, I try to keep my own face expressionless as they run through a list of who might have been killed by Ethan and why. It's clearly not Daphne, the winsome blonde wife of Ethan's former college roommate, because she's the one who finds a body in the sea in the first five minutes of the show. Nor is it the blunt hotel manager, Valentina, who steps out of a hotel shuttle into the chaos of first responders shouting into walkie-talkies and carrying body bags from the beach to the waiting ambulances. "I think we should watch an episode or two this evening," my mother says. "We need more information."

The check comes, and that's when I notice the plaque on the wall next to me. It reads "*SIDEWAYS*: Scene #5, Breakfast, Filmed in this booth October 2003, Solvang Restaurant, Solvang, California."

What were the chances

Sideways was released on DVD in 2005, and David and I watched it the following year on a laptop in bed over a period of several weeks in approximately ten-minute increments.

The movie arrived at our house sometime that fall, in a red envelope bearing the inscription *Netflix* (Netflix: founded in Silicon Valley in 1997). David and I were working full-time; En was four, and her two older brothers–let's use their camp names and call them Nemo and Orion–were six and ten.

We watched *Sideways* in bed prior to going to sleep because that was the only quiet time we had, and as we were perpetually exhausted, both by our jobs and by our children, we would begin dozing off approximately ten minutes into each viewing. Occasionally we'd miss a couple of nights because one of the kids was sick, or because we were too tired, and every once in a while, we'd forget what we watched and rewatch the previous ten-minute segment. *Sideways* is not fast-paced–almost none of Alexander Payne's films are–but our drawn-out viewing finally culminated in a heroic effort to stay awake for nineteen minutes straight, so eager were we to discover how, or whether, the tangled narrative line would unravel.

Sideways is about two friends on a road trip through the Santa Ynez Valley. They traverse almost exactly the same terrain as my mother, En, and I were traversing now, except for the fact that they drove in from Southern California and we drove in from the north. Miles is a divorced English teacher, an unpublished novelist, and an oenophile; his friend Jack is a voice actor about to marry into money. Miles thinks the purpose of the trip is to taste wine; Jack thinks the purpose of the trip is to get laid before getting married. As soon as they set out, Miles insists on detouring to Oxnard to his mother's house where he steals money from her wallet to fund the trip. They have dinner at a Buellton restaurant called The Hitching Post. Jack sleeps with a woman who breaks his nose after she discovers he's engaged; the following night, he runs naked from the house of another woman whose husband catches him in flagrante with his wife and gives chase. On the way back to LA, Jack crashes Miles's car into a tree to reconcile the truth of his broken nose (infidelity) with the story he's planning to tell his fiancée about how he broke his nose (car crash). It's sad and comical and confusing, and En seems mostly unimpressed by our explanation of why the movie was so good except for the mention of Sandra Oh, whose performance in *Killing Eve* she idolizes.

"What a charming movie, *Sideways*," my mother says. "And what were the chances that we would end up in this very restaurant and they would put us in this exact booth?"

"Okay, but also," En says, "can we talk about Portia's stupid nail polish?" (Portia's nail polish is an unpleasant yellow-green that we all agree was supposed to complement her blue-green-yellow vest but doesn't.) "And I thought it was so funny in that scene by the pool where Portia was like, 'I went to Chico State,' and Albie was all, 'Cool,' and she was like, 'Yeah, cool.' How hilarious was that?"

Depends on who you ask

Orion, our middle son, attended Chico State for a year. He went there mostly because David and I assumed that everyone goes to college after high school, and he was affable and pliant, so off he went. He lived in honors housing, because we bulldozed him to apply to the honors college, and for the first month or two, he seemed to be doing well. He even sent me a draft of a paper he was writing for his humanities seminar about Ovid's *Metamorphoses.* The draft was pretty good. Even though he had never been particularly enthusiastic about school, college was going to transform him. I was sure of it. It would make him into someone else–someone with a college degree, someone with forward momentum, someone . . . bolder.

When our children were little, I used to joke that if we had a staircase (we didn't; our house was single story), our oldest and youngest would hurl themselves down headfirst to get to the bottom as quickly as they could. Our middle son, on the other hand, would come down sideways, one hand on the banister, planting one careful foot at a time on each tread. (This was how he descended actual stairs until he was almost ten.) "So funny how all kids are different, and thank God for at least one cautious kid, right?" I would say. But then, when he came home from college and sat on the couch wrapped in a blanket and didn't go anywhere, it didn't seem funny at all.

Like this, you do not have

Morning Solvang is more welcoming than nighttime Solvang–quaint storefronts and windmills and sunlight glinting on steep copper roofs. We stop in a hat shop on our way back to the car and try on cowboy hats and fancy hats with feathers and veils and a plastic helmet with Viking horns and two blonde braids attached to either side. "You should definitely get that," En says to me when I put it on, and my mother nods and says, "*Takovo u tebya nyet*"–like this, you do not have.

"Like this, you do not have" was one of Grandma Ester's favorite phrases, deployed as a means of persuasion whenever she and I went to Ross Dress for Less, a discount clothing store near her apartment in Palo Alto. She would find a dress she thought might look good on me, or a sweater, or a blouse, and if I protested that I already had something similar, she retorted, "*Takovo u tebya nyet*," like this, you do not have. Other favorite phrases included "*Yazyk moy, vrag moy*"–my tongue is my enemy–used whenever she said something hurtful or tactless, which was often, and "*Kak ty menya rastroila*"–you've upset me terribly.

Grandma Ester was upset by many things–being unable to reach me or my mother by phone, finding out that someone was sick, weight loss beyond what she considered appropriate, learning that an academic article I published in *The Henry James Review* was compensated only by complimentary copies of the issue in which the article appeared–and unlike quiet, self-contained Grandma Tsilya, she made her displeasure known. She was mercurial and bombastic and imperious. When I was little, she raged and stormed like King Lear on the heath when my cousin Inna and I giggled at the table, calling us morons and threatening to upend the bowls of soup on our heads and/or to lock us in the bathroom with our plates of food. Five minutes later, she would shower us with kisses and tell us how much she loved us.

En was fifteen when Grandma Ester died. She remembers an elderly woman who moved slowly and used a walker and furtively handed out Hershey's bars before dinner. She remembers Grandma Ester's vast collection of miniature shoes–tiny wooden clogs from Holland, glass boots from Italy, cowboy boots from Texas, dainty porcelain slippers, brightly painted plastic tennis shoes, ceramic stilettos. Thousands of them.

Like most collections, Grandma Ester's began by chance after she brought back souvenir shoes from a trip, maybe even wooden clogs from Solvang. After that, everyone who knew her decided that miniature shoes were her thing. So many of them, flowing in year after year, long after she stopped buying them herself. After she died, we couldn't bear to throw them away, but no one knew what to do with them. Such a small, innocuous act, buying a pair of souvenir shoes. Who would have thought it would take on such weight, become such a burden?

Best practices

We're back on westbound Highway 246 on our way to Ostrich-land USA, each of us full of aebleskiver and our own thoughts, when En pipes up from the back seat.

"Mom," she says, "do you know the best piece of advice you've ever given me?"

I rack my brain. All I can think of is stupidly obvious: Take your makeup off before bed, tip generously, use "fewer" when referring to things that can be counted and "less" when referring to things that cannot.

"Tell me," I say.

"Don't brake-check if someone is tailgating you," En announces triumphantly, "because you never know who has a gun."

I have no recollection of ever sharing this particular piece of wisdom with her, but being on alert for the worst possible outcome seems pretty on brand for me, and as far as advice goes, it's not my worst.

Sage counsel

The *Odyssey* is a book about the eponymous voyage, but it begins with a smaller, lesser-known trip: In the opening chapters of the *Odyssey*, Odysseus's son Telemachus leaves Ithaca for Pylos and Sparta to seek news of his missing father. Telemachus's mother, Penelope–besieged by brash suitors vying for her hand in marriage, beset by worry for her absent husband–is reluctant to let her only son go. But Telemachus has been advised by none other than the goddess Athena herself, and he can no longer bear to sit around waiting and wondering and watching the suitors devour his father's cattle and drain his father's wine, so he sets sail.

The *Odyssey* is full of advice, some of it followed, some of it ignored. The seer Tiresias advises Odysseus to keep an eye on his men and to exercise caution when he returns home; Aeolus, the god of wind, instructs him not to open the bag in which all the winds except for the gentle homeward breeze have been contained; the shade of the murdered Agamemnon warns him to "trust a woman never / and never tell her all you know"; Circe cautions Odysseus against listening to the Sirens' song. When his ship comes to the narrow passage between Scylla and Charybdis, she tells him to steer closer to Scylla, a six-headed, snake-necked monster who devours men, rather than Charybdis, a yawning whirlpool that swallows ships whole. Better to lose some of the crew than the entire ship.

My family's term for unsolicited advice is "*tsenniye ukazaniye*"—valuable directions—a phrase typically delivered with a generous helping of sarcasm. As in, *thanks for your input* (but not really). My grandmothers would advise my parents to do something or not to do something, or my parents would advise me to do something or not to do something (take the CB radio, why do you have cigarettes in your backpack, you should be getting better grades, that's too much eyeliner, your room is a pigsty, we would have never let you get away with it if you behaved the way your children behave), and I would either take the advice or ignore it. But I hardly ever pushed back. That wasn't our way. Soviet parents gave valuable directions and Soviet children followed the directions, or they didn't, but if they didn't, they disobeyed quietly. I excelled at quiet defiance. I snuck around. I avoided conflict. It took me over thirty years to tell my father that Leslie and I had no idea how to use the CB radio back in 1987, although even then, I appreciated that he wanted us to be safe.

Birds of prey

It's the smell that hits us first: acrid, thick, meaty. We can smell it in the gift shop, which sells ostrich-skin purses and belts and hats; when we walk out to the pasture, where the ostriches are clustered alongside a wooden fence with widely spaced horizontal slats, the stench hits us like a sledgehammer.

The ostriches have long, undulating, serpentine necks and coldly calculating eyes and an air of ancient menace. To feed them, you extend a bowl with a long handle and they dip their heads through the fence and attack the dry pellets inside the bowl with so much focused belligerence that we shriek and jump back even though we're out of their reach. The signs say not to reach through the fence or pet the ostriches, which we have no plans of doing because they are utterly, completely terrifying.

The three of us laugh and grimace and shriek as the ostriches devour their food and angle their heads, now one way, now another, seemingly intent on doing harm. "They are just like the cassowary in Australia!" En says. "You think they're going to be so cool but then you get closer and they're, like, murderous."

"The smell," says my mother, "is giving me a headache."

After fifteen minutes, we decide that we're done with the ostriches. En waves to them as we leave and calls out, "Bye, hanischkas, bye!"

My aunt Klara had a phrase to describe people like us: "not a friend of animals."

Dirty and dangerous

The sky is a translucent blue. The sun is shining like yesterday's deluge never happened, and we've discarded our jackets and rolled down the car windows. We've decided not to take northbound 101 to Los Olivos, even though it's the faster, more direct route, because we've already been on 101. Instead, we take eastbound 246, a one-lane, gently curving highway that runs past farms and pastures and green hills dotted with yellow wood sorrel. This is *Sideways* country, which En doesn't care about because she hasn't seen the movie, but she agrees that it's pretty.

Every parking spot in front of Bob's Well Bread is full, and I wedge our car into a tight spot on a side street. "Can we all please appreciate my masterful parallel parking skills?" I say to my mother and En, because I suddenly feel diminished–practically irrelevant–after heroically steering the three of us through yesterday's storm. "Yes, yay, good job," En says perfunctorily, and my mother says, "Wow, amazing!" and I roll my eyes at both of them.

At Bob's Well Bread, we find a table outside and eat avocado toast and drink almond milk cappuccinos and discuss who in our family was a friend of animals and who wasn't.

Grandma Tsilya was convinced that all animals were dirty and dangerous. To prove her point, she invariably brought up What Happened to Boris When He Was a Baby. What happened was that my grandmother left my father's younger brother in his bassinet for half a minute to get something from another room and when she returned, he was red-faced and struggling to breathe.

"I left a healthy baby, sound asleep, and came back to this–" she would say, and gesture broadly to indicate the catastrophic, bewildering magnitude of "this." The mystery was solved when she pulled back baby Boris's blanket and discovered a big black cat curled up on his chest. Somehow, the cat had managed to sneak in through an open window, slither under the baby blanket, and evade detection until the moment of dramatic discovery.

Whenever Grandma Tsilya told this story, Aunt Klara–an inveterate petter of dogs and feeder of stray cats–would say, "Tsilya, you are not a friend of animals," and my grandmother would look at her like *I know what I saw.*

"Speaking of animals," I add, "did I ever tell you about the time that Babushka flung her wedding ring into the gorilla pit at the Rome Zoo?"

The time my mother flung her wedding ring into the gorilla pit at the Rome Zoo

Rome was our last stop before entering the United States. Rome was where thousands of Soviet émigrés waited for their requests for political asylum to be approved by the US government. Rome was where my parents and I lived in a four-bedroom apartment with two other Soviet families and a wizened, cantankerous landlady named Maria. The apartment had tall ceilings, cold marble floors, and a small kitchen where women bumped into each other and where Maria zealously monitored who used the gas stove and for how long because gas was expensive.

In October of 1977, my parents and I paid a visit to the Rome Zoo, where we strolled around and looked at the animals. Eventually, we stopped to rest on a bench near the gorilla enclosure—a deep stone basin with some artfully scattered rocks among which sat some bored-looking, artfully scattered gorillas.

We had bought fruit that morning, and my mother was eating an apple. On her right hand were two rings—the oval malachite ring and a heavy gold band, which was technically two gold wedding bands smelted together—one hers, one my father's—because the Soviet Union placed stringent limits on what émigrés could take when they left the country, including the number of rings. The apple was red and juicy; between bites, my mother expounded on how much she disliked zoos, how seeing animals in captivity made her sad. When the apple was finished, she flung the apple core toward a wastebasket positioned right in front of the gorilla enclosure and the apple core sailed straight into the basket, but the heavy gold band on her left hand (which was loose, partly because immigration is stressful and causes weight loss and partly because her fingers were slick with apple juice) continued to sail elegantly past the wastebasket and over the railing and right into the gorilla enclosure.

For a moment, we were too stunned to move. Then, as one, we rushed to the railing. The gorillas were no longer bored; they were now eager to investigate the small shiny object that dropped from the heavens into their midst. They passed it around and examined it; one of them tasted it to see if it was edible, provoking a dismayed shriek from my mother, who was no longer sad about seeing animals in captivity.

We found a man in a zoo uniform and my father managed to explain what had happened with the help of pantomime and a Russian–Italian dictionary. After the zoo employee stopped laughing, he disappeared into a small structure near the enclosure and a minute later reappeared among the gorillas down below. He removed a banana from his pocket, extended it toward the gorilla whose turn it was to hold the ring, made the exchange, and returned the ring to my mother.

I've told the story about my mother's wedding band and the gorillas at the Rome Zoo many times. Once, my father overheard me and cut in to set the record straight: Before the zoo employee rescued my mother's ring, he called over six or seven colleagues and they all had a good laugh while the three of us stood there, waiting. My father does not remember anything about the banana.

Speaking of rings

I'm finishing my avocado toast when En points to my right hand and says, "Let me see."

She's referring to a ring on the middle finger of my right hand. The ring is silver, with a pale-green oval stone set in a slim bezel. My father bought it for me on a trip to New York in 2012, where we traveled because an essay I had written about watching TV and eating Kellogg's Corn Pops when we first came to America was selected for publication in an anthology of poems and stories by Soviet émigrés about leaving the USSR or arriving in the US, or living in the in-between (Austria, Italy). There was a big event to celebrate the launch of the anthology, with a reception and speakers, and even though I wasn't asked to be a speaker, all the contributors would be recognized. The event was in the middle of the week and David couldn't take time off work, and someone needed to stay home with our three children anyway, and my parents said they would be delighted to go with me. It would be like old times, just the three of us.

We ate in a restaurant whose lobby was lined with shallow wooden shelves and every shelf had apples lined up on it, rows and rows of them, with a fragrance so intoxicating that walking into the lobby of the restaurant felt like stepping into an orchard. Or like stepping back in time to the dacha in Luzanovka–the fragrance of sun-warmed fruit, the dappled light. We visited the

Tenement Museum, where an apartment preserved to look like it did in the 1890s had a table with an old Singer sewing machine by the window, and we wondered out loud what Grandma Tsilya could have done if she came to America as a little girl, how she might have parlayed her gift for sewing into a sartorial empire. We ate bagels and lox at Russ & Daughters, an iconic Lower East Side shop selling every variety of smoked fish that I learned about after reading Calvin Trillin, whose grandparents also came to the United States from Russia, but in a boat, not on a plane. My parents and I had been in the US for thirty-four years at that point, but we had never talked–really talked–about the full shape of our story. One of the speakers at the event had written a book called *When They Come for Us, We'll Be Gone*–a comprehensive history of Soviet-Jewish emigration in the 1970s–and he spoke about the political pressure American Jews exerted on the Carter administration to make Soviet Jewry a human rights issue. Much of that activism, he said, had been driven by guilt of not speaking up, of not doing enough to help European Jews flee Europe and find refuge in the United States during the Second World War. We had not known any of this because we were on the inside, cut off from the rest of the world. We did not know that Jewish teens in the US were twinned with Jewish teens in the Soviet Union as part of their bar and bat mitzvah preparations and wrote letters and went to rallies, and we chewed our bagels and talked about how much we didn't know, and how much the Jews in America didn't know, and how my parents' biggest regret was not leaving earlier.

Then we walked to our hotel, past a line of vendors selling watches, handbags, I ❤ NY T-shirts, and silver rings, and I spotted the ring I wanted, suddenly, urgently, on one of the trays lined with black velvet. It was silver, with a flat, pale-green, bezel-set stone. There was a white inclusion in the stone–a crack deep inside, or maybe a sliver of another rock or mineral–and because of that I wanted it even more. There was something about the color that drew me; the color had a name and I couldn't think of it. "Thirty dollars," the vendor said. I reached for my wallet but my father moved me aside gently and said, "Twenty." My mother caught my eye and said the Russian equivalent of "You can take the boy out of Odesa, but you can't take Odesa out of the boy." My father bought the ring for twenty-four dollars and handed it to me. It fit perfectly on the middle finger of my right hand. The color of the stone came to me later that day, as we were eating dinner and laughing about how my mother and I thought we were millionaires after a Publishers Clearing House Sweepstakes envelope arrived in the mail during our early days in San Francisco. We didn't yet understand conditional verbs, and we took "You may already be a winner" as fact, not possibility.

The color I was thinking of was celadon, a pale green with gray undertones.

I take the ring off, and as En reaches for it, I tell her that you're not supposed to give a ring directly to someone unless you're getting married. Rather, you're supposed to place it on a surface between you, where the other person can pick it up. I learned this from my friend Lilya who emigrated from Moscow with her parents at the same age I did, only a year later. I don't know the reason for this particular superstition, but I believe in an abundance of caution.

A very partial list of Russian superstitions, all of which I believe

If you spill salt, toss a pinch of it over your left shoulder and spit three times lest there be a quarrel in the family. When you pour someone a cup of tea, fill it to the brim to ensure they'll have a full life.

There is, always, the omnipresent threat of the evil eye. The Russian word *sglazit'* means to cast a dark glance at someone's luck and ruin everything. Both my grandmothers were vigilant in guarding against the evil eye. Spit three times over your left shoulder. Downplay your good luck; shrug ostentatiously at your children's and grandchildren's successes. Don't draw attention to yourself. If someone else praises the people you love, put your thumb between your middle and index fingers and make a fist in your pocket.

My precious

The funny thing, I tell En as she examines my ring, is that ring-flinging might be hereditary.

The summer after we graduated from high school, David invited me to go hiking at a local nature preserve. Unbeknownst to me, he brought a picnic lunch (Babybel cheese and Hi-C juice boxes), and as we ate our lunch in a meadow, he said, “I found the ring you lost in my car,” and handed me the cheap jade ring I got in Chinatown and lost in his car because a) it was too big and b) I gesticulate dramatically when I talk.

I had not yet read *The Hobbit* or *The Lord of the Rings*, because I didn’t grow up in America. I knew about Baba Yaga, but not about Bilbo Baggins or Frodo or rings with a will of their own. Before I could thank David, he handed me a small box and said, “And I got you another ring to go with it.” Inside the box was a simple silver ring, and I was completely undone because no one had ever given me a ring before and I was already pretty sure that I was eating Babybel cheese and drinking Hi-C fruit punch with the love of my life.

There was only one problem: He used the too-big jade ring as a sizing guide, and the silver ring was also too big, and as we walked back holding hands, I gestured dramatically to make a point, and the ring flew into the undergrowth. We searched for it for almost an hour and eventually gave up, discouraged. As we walked back in strained silence, I thought, *Shit shit shit, he will never give me another ring again.*

Mazel tov

Four years later–almost to the day–we got married in a lavish ceremony in San Francisco, in the Gold Room of the Fairmont Hotel. My parents took out a second mortgage to pay for the wedding. I wore a cream-colored dress that looked like a nineteenth-century ball gown–nipped at the waist, puff sleeves, lace, illusion netting covering my arms and chest, and a long embroidered train that bustled into a complicated construction in the back for dancing. It came with an equally elaborate veil that descended from a pearl-encrusted headpiece and almost caught fire from the candles on our table when David and I posed for photos during dinner.

When Grandma Ester and Grandma Tsilya saw me in the dress, they gasped and fell into each other's arms. "Tsilya Borisovna, mazel tov," Grandma Ester said tearily.

"Mazel tov" is a congratulatory Yiddish phrase, but less of a wish than a statement of fact, like "Good luck has occurred."

I was the first granddaughter to get married, and to get married well. (A Jewish boy, from a good family! A future doctor!) Before the wedding, both grandmothers had been worried, and not subtly, about my purity. Who dated the same boy for four years without getting married? It didn't matter that David and I were only twenty-one, that we attended college on opposite sides of the country, that our courtship was mostly chaste and mostly epistolary, that whenever I stayed at David's parents' house or he stayed at mine we were assigned separate bedrooms. My reputation was at serious risk. People were talking. Which people, and what they might be saying, no one knew, but it was imperative not to become the subject of gossip. Anyway, I was now a bride, my reputation was safe, I was safe. Grandma Tsilya examined the stitching on the dress, the silk-covered buttons in the back, the pearl beading, the lace, and nodded approvingly. Mazel tov.

I had wanted a different dress, but several months before the wedding, I developed hives–large, angry-looking welts that periodically erupted out of nowhere, like a curse, all over my neck and chest and arms. I went to a dermatologist, who shrugged and said something about avoiding stress. Since being the center of attention at a lavish wedding with 150 people in attendance was not a good way to avoid stress, my wedding dress had to camouflage my possible disfigurement. Illusion netting to provide the illusion that everything was as it should be.

The dress I wanted was an off-the-shoulder sheath, sleeveless, simple, with a veil that was nothing more than a length of tulle that fell from a silk bow at the back of the head. It was the nuptial equivalent of the black velvet gown Anna Karenina wears to the Moscow ball where Vronsky falls in love with her–devastatingly simple, restrained, elegant. What I got was the equivalent of Kitty Scherbatsky's dress–a frothy confection for a naive debutante, except ivory instead of pink.

I never got hives at the wedding, but how was I supposed to know that what we prepared for wouldn't happen? Or that what we hadn't prepared for would?

Write it down in your little books

In *Roadside America*, Mr. Adams, who serves as translator and guide for Ilf and Petrov on their cross-country trip, periodically makes weighty pronouncements and observations and tells his listeners half-jokingly and half not, "*Zapishite v vashi knizhechki*"—write it down in your little books.

After more than forty years in the United States, my parents and I speak a Russian that's preserved in amber from the day we left: September 17, 1977. We salt it with English words, more and more every year, because they come more easily than Russian ones, and because words like *credit card*, *microwave*, *traffic*, and *homeowner's insurance* didn't exist in Russian when we left. We don't know the latest slang. I only recently learned from a manicurist who emigrated from Russia in 2015 how to say "cool" in Russian—*kruto*, which literally means "steep." But the phrase from a travelogue written in 1937—"write it down in your little books"—is forever part of my parents' and my shared vocabulary. Whenever something noteworthy, or not even particularly noteworthy happens, one of us will say, "*Zapishite v vashi knizhechki*."

I don't usually write on trips. I write after the fact. Except during the two weeks in Vienna after my parents and I left the USSR, when I chronicled what we saw—the Natural History Museum, the Schönbrunn Palace, a courtyard festooned with hanging lights–in a small notebook with a mottled magenta cover. In the summer of 1986, right before I left for college, my parents and my friend Lilya's parents rented an economy-sized van and drove from the San Francisco Bay Area to Vancouver, Canada, to see the World Expo. Lilya and I sat in the very back and made fun of our parents in a combination of English and Russian, and I faithfully transcribed everything everyone said and everything we saw in a college-ruled, spiral-bound notebook as Lilya peered over my shoulder and snickered appreciatively.

I have, however, kept diaries for most of my life. I started keeping a diary after I read *The Diary of Anne Frank*, in a Russian translation, because we had just arrived in San Francisco and I did not yet speak English. I wrote, sporadically, in Russian, chronicling what happened during the day, what I ate, who was mean to me at school (everyone). In sixth grade, I shifted to English. At some point, it occurred to me that writing was a talisman against oblivion, that someday I would die but my words would live on. Months would go by without an entry, and then the new entry would invariably start with an apology for not writing, a lament for how much was lost and would now never be recalled. Long, breathless passages with promises to write more, to write regularly, followed by long periods of not writing. In eighth grade, a brief entry: "Mom was being such a bitch today. She kept yelling at me because she said I was using 'that tone of voice.' I don't know what she was talking about. I was using a totally normal tone of voice."

A few months before we left on our trip, I wanted to show En that entry, but I couldn't find the diary. I still can't.

"*Zapishite v vashi knizhechki*," says my mother. "That was an excellent second breakfast."

Part 2

BAGGAGE CLAIM

January 6: Los Olivos–Paso Robles

I just feel like there must have been a time when the world had more. You know? Like . . . mystery or . . . or something . . . and you can't even get lost anymore 'cause you can just find yourself on Google Maps.

–Portia, *The White Lotus*

America is not a place; it is a road.

–Landon Jones,
"On the Trail of Nabokov in the American West"

Record-keeping

Grandma Tsilya had quick, agile hands and a quick, agile mind. By the time she was eight, she was fluent in Russian, Ukrainian, and Hebrew in addition to the Yiddish she spoke with her family. After the revolution, after Ukraine was sutured onto the Union of Soviet Socialist Republics, she showed a classmate how Hebrew was written from right to left, not left to right like Russian, and the next day her father was summoned to her school and informed that if his daughter spoke or wrote in Hebrew again she would be taken from the home. That evening, my great-grandfather told her to forget everything she learned.

Like her stitches, Grandma Tsilya's stories were neat, tight, carefully spaced. Grandma Ester was more forthcoming, but she broke down whenever she mentioned her firstborn or her parents–her brilliant, erudite, volatile father; her gentle, accommodating, gracious mother. Occasionally she tried to describe her mother's renowned dumplings, or the scent of homemade challah on Shabbat, and her eyes would grow distant, and then she would stop talking and wave her hand mid-sentence as though to chase away the memories. I didn't press for more because I didn't want to pry, and now that both grandmothers are gone, I wonder whether my questions could have hurt them any more than they had already been hurt.

Recently, my father told me another story about the evacuation to Kirov: One especially cold winter morning, Grandma Tsilya went out to get milk and fell through a deep snowdrift. The snow reached above her head. She would have perished there, a frozen exclamation mark, but a passerby heard her screaming for help and pulled her out. I imagine her after being rescued, continuing on to get milk, leaving a line of careful footprints on the snow. I imagine her telling my father this story years later, measured, matter-of-fact.

My father, who was four when they returned to Odesa, remembers Kirov only as a patch of grass, a well he was forbidden to approach, a wall covered with raspberry shoots.

En has tried to track down our family history online. She has found almost nothing. The war leveled towns and destroyed archives; after the war, the Soviet government excised whatever was left. *Excise*: a word that sounds like a seam being ripped out, like the hiss of scissors through fabric.

In my dissertation, I drew on psychoanalytic theory to argue that language is born of loss, that we spend our lives trying to evoke what we no longer have. Words are an imperfect substitute–just as often, they point to an absence, not a presence–but in the end, they're all we have. Except that sometimes, people who have lost everything don't want to talk about it.

Sandpipers

All three of us are stuffed. In addition to the avocado toast, we've ordered several croissants, just to try. "Just to try" is what En and I say to my mother after she raises her eyebrows at what she perceives to be our gluttony. My mother does not condone gluttony. I explain that it's really in the interest of scientific research, since I consider it my obligation to compare Bay Area croissants to Central Coast croissants.

Now, my mother gestures at the mostly untouched croissants and says, "I told you."

I ask the cashier for a to-go bag and tell my mother that she'll thank me later. Then we get back on northbound 101, toward Paso Robles.

But forty minutes into our drive, the Pacific appears on our left, cobalt blue and sparkling behind rows of palm trees, and we decide to stop in Avila Beach. The sand is strewn with storm debris–splintered wood, tangled strands of bullwhip kelp with their strange, bulbous ends. Along the water, sandpipers skitter on the wet sand, leaving arrowhead-shaped footprints that vanish as soon as a new wave rolls in. I try to take a picture, but the sandpipers are too small and the ocean is too big and they dart out of the frame every time I line up the shot.

Writing is like that. The ideas dart out of the frame. The words scatter. The story itself is so simple: car, rain, road, hotel, television show, coffee, ostriches. But then the past rolls in and the car fills with clamorous ghosts. The ghosts want to be part of the story. If I don't let them in, the story becomes a travelogue. I want this story to mean something more, something beyond *We went here, we saw that.*

In Book XI of the *Odyssey*, Odysseus and his men sail to the edge of the known world so they can visit the underworld. In that sunless realm, Odysseus summons the "blurred and breathless dead," first pouring out milk, honey, wine, and water and then sacrificing a ram and a ewe. The murmuring souls gather around the spilled blood, the old and the young, "tender girls whose hearts were new to grief," warriors "torn by brazen lanceheads, / battle-slain, bearing still their bloody gear." Then, one by one, they speak. Odysseus sees his mother, Anticlea, and learns that she died of grief during his long absence. The seer Tiresias warns him about the insolent suitors courting his wife and devouring his livestock back home on Ithaca. The ghost of Agamemnon instructs him never to indulge a woman and never to tell her all he knows. Their words weigh Odysseus down, like stones.

Along the Avila Beach boardwalk, a low, semicircular stone bench curves around a colorful tile floor inlay. According to a nearby sign, the inlay–titled "The Circle of Life"–was created by local artists to represent the history of Avila Beach: original Chumash settlements, pier, fishing, lighthouse, catastrophic 1992 oil spill, restoration.

It's clear to my mother and En and me that the so-called circle is actually a spiral–a continuous unfurling line of dark-blue, yellow-crested waves against a salmon and light-blue background, curving around and around in widening circles. The pivotal historical moments are tiny mosaic icons perched on the outer edges. They look like footnotes, like distant relatives huddled forlornly on the sidelines of an extravagant wedding. The stylized waves look like the waves on ancient Greek pottery, only jewel-bright instead of black and orange.

"You know what's missing?" my mother asks, and steps into the center of the spiral, lifting one arm theatrically and tilting her chin down. "A statue!"

I take a picture. My mother looks lithe and audacious, her auburn bob flaming in the sun, the tiles blazing blue and salmon-pink and yellow around her. En yells, "My turn!" and strikes a pose in the place my mother has vacated. Then the three of us take a selfie, and this time we are all looking in the same direction and we look happy and the sun is shining, so I text the photo to David and write, "Avila Beach, en route to Paso Robles. So far, so good."

So far, so good

At my Soviet elementary school, my teacher called me a *vyskochka*, which literally translates to "someone who jumps ahead," because my father taught me cursive and multiplication at home ahead of my class. Soviet children were supposed to march in lockstep, as a collective, and jumping ahead was frowned upon. But my father wanted to jump ahead, and he wanted me to jump ahead, and that was the main reason we came to America.

America was a place for people who wanted to take big leaps, to go big or go home. (Going home was not an option for us, which left going big.) Unlike the Soviet Union, where you advanced by not being Jewish, knowing which people to bribe, and having enough to bribe those people, America was a meritocracy, where everyone had the same opportunities and the spoils went to whoever worked the hardest. It was simple and elegant and enticing.

California, the golden state that became our new home, was built by people who knew an opportunity when they saw one. The San Francisco waterfront rests on the skeletons of sunken ships that were abandoned by passengers and crew who rushed inland to prospect for gold after general store owner Sam Brannan paraded down Market Street in 1848 shouting, "Gold! Gold in the American River!" Just across the bay, in Alameda, the westernmost terminus of the transcontinental railroad began receiving passengers in 1869, and in 1875, Leland Stanford, the president of the company that built the transcontinental railroad, began breeding the finest, fastest racehorses on an 11,000-acre farm that later became Stanford University. In 1939, two Stanford graduates named Bill Hewlett and David Packard started making electronic oscillators in a Palo Alto garage. Soon after, technology companies, some of them with mythical names–Oracle, Apple–began to replace fruit orchards and farms, and the place known as the Valley of Heart's Delight became known by a new name: Silicon Valley.

Soon after our arrival in San Francisco, my father, who spoke reasonably good English, found work as an engineer; my mother, who did not speak much English, enrolled in college courses so she could also become an engineer. For a brief and bumpy stretch, I was the stick in the wheel of our progress: I didn't speak any English, but I understood enough to know that my fourth-grade classmates were making fun of me, and every evening I sobbed furiously and accused my parents of ruining my life by bringing me to this stupid country instead of staying in Moscow, where I had been weeks away from becoming a young Pioneer and receiving a coveted scarlet scarf to wear around my neck.

My parents promised me that soon, I would learn to speak English so well that I would correct their mistakes, and although I didn't believe them at first, it turned out I was wrong and they were right. I learned to speak English. My father did not work as a plumber or electrician. My mother did not walk the streets. They bought a car and furniture and a color television and a house in Sunnyvale. They returned to San Francisco seventeen years after they bought their house in Sunnyvale, only instead of an apartment on a noisy street corner upstairs from a Japanese restaurant whose sign blinked purple and pink into the bedroom window, they moved into an apartment in a high-rise on a hill with a view of the Golden Gate Bridge. I majored in

English and got a PhD in comparative literature and married and had three children.

In the early '90s, my father and his brother, my uncle Boris, leased a bare-bones office at the east edge of Palo Alto and founded a telecom start-up. In the photos, they look young and eager and hungry–their sleeves rolled up, their ties loosened like an afterthought. They created a device that compressed voice and data signals in order to transmit them more quickly over multiple channels through a single physical phone line; four years later, their start-up went public and the windfall was such that my parents were able to help David and me to buy a house in Palo Alto. So far, so good, so fast, and best of all, there was no reason to believe that our good fortune wouldn't continue.

Finders keepers

En has a knack for finding treasures online–memes and TikToks and reels that are absurd and oblique and hilarious and eminently quotable. In one of the videos, a man is banging on the plate glass window of a bank shouting, "Why are your doors closed to the public?" while people walk through automated sliding doors ten feet away from him.

She also has a prehensile memory for song lyrics, in the same way that I have a prehensile memory for passages from books I've read. We're good at finding things, the two of us–a quality we probably inherited from my father, who draws lost objects like a magnet–an iron nail, likely centuries old, on the Appian Way in Rome; an oversized watch with a square face and a studded black leather band on the sand near Aquatic Park in San Francisco; a lost cell phone with an operating system entirely in Japanese, which he managed to decipher so that he could reach the owner.

When I was in graduate school, I bought a ring from one of the many jewelry stands around LA's Westwood Village. The ring was oxidized silver, with a round, veined, dark-red stone set into a filigree bezel. The stone was likely plastic, but it looked real–a passable imitation of carnelian. One morning, while preparing to teach my introductory humanities class, I looked down at my hand and saw that the stone had fallen out; where it should have been was an empty space containing nothing but a small metal spiral to which the bottom of the stone had been glued. I had walked from my apartment in Westwood all the way across campus, at least two miles, and the stone could have fallen out anywhere. I slid the emptied ring in my pocket, taught my class, went to my Edith Wharton seminar, and then walked back to my apartment, head down, scanning the ground for the stone as though it were a given that I would come across a tiny red hemisphere somewhere on a huge college campus traversed by tens of thousands of people daily.

I found it while walking through the Engineering Quad on South Campus, about a mile from where I was when I first realized the stone was missing. At first I thought my eyes were playing tricks on me, but there it was, just lying there like it was waiting for me all this time. It felt like a sign. I was lucky; I was special; I could will something improbable into being.

En discovered the phrase "Why is this happening to me, a mostly good person?" in an online Harry Potter series featuring stills from the movies paired with flippant, satirical captions. "Why is this happening to me, a mostly good person?" was the caption that described Dumbledore's exasperation when Harry's name is pulled from the Goblet of Fire at the Triwizard Tournament because Dumbledore keeps trying to protect Harry and Harry, in spite of Dumbledore's best efforts, keeps ending up in dangerous situations. The phrase has entered our family lexicon. It's the qualifier at the end—*a mostly good person*—that does it for me. I mean, aren't most of us mostly good people?

For several years now, En has tried to track down the series to show me the quote, to prove that it exists, that she did not make it up—to no avail. She even tried invoking Saint Anthony, the patron saint of lost objects, but no trace of it remains.

During the course of her search, En learned that whatever can't be tracked down on the Internet is called lost media. When she told me this, I widened my eyes at her as if to say, *Seriously?*

and she widened her eyes back at me as if to say, *I know*. Neither one of us can understand how something that originated online can be lost. Isn't everything on the Internet eternal? Isn't that what technology is for? To connect us, to keep us on course, to help us remember what we might forget?

Why is this happening to me, a mostly good person?

North of Avila Beach, Highway 101 turns away from the Pacific and winds through the coastal redwoods, Pacific madrones, and ponderosa pines that cover the Santa Lucia Mountains. Over the course of our drive north, we've discussed the whaling chapters in *Moby-Dick*, which En has just finished reading in her American literature class, and the creepy Moor head sculptures scattered throughout the White Lotus hotel. Now, we're discussing Aunt Klara and Uncle Isaak and their incessant, comprehensive bickering.

Aunt Klara died before En was born and Uncle Isaak died when she was a baby. "I wish I had gotten to meet them," En says now. "But why did they argue so much?"

I explain that arguing was their love language, like Miracle Max and Valerie in *The Princess Bride*. "Actually, they were the kindest, most generous, most hospitable people ever," I tell En. "And Aunt Klara was an amazing cook. After she died, I still had some strudel she had made, and I wrapped it in tinfoil and kept it in our freezer for years. I know it's weird, but I wanted to have something she had touched with her hands."

"I totally get that," En says.

We're quiet for a few minutes, and then En breaks the silence. "Question about the two rich couples vacationing together on

The White Lotus," she says. "I don't understand why the couple where the wife feels like they're LARPing as rich people would be going to Italy with the obnoxious rich couple. Just because the husbands were college roommates?"

"At Yale," I respond. "Don't forget they both went to Yale. You know who else went to Yale? Tom Buchanan in *The Great Gatsby*."

En snorts and says, "Yeah, that tracks."

"What is LARPing?" my mother asks. "I forgot to ask before."

LARPing is an acronym for live-action role-play, where players dress up as characters from a particular genre or time period–science fiction, fantasy, the Renaissance–and play assigned parts in a pre-scripted narrative. A graduate student in my program spent nearly every weekend LARPing in nearby parks with a group devoted to all things medieval. Her boyfriend made his own chain mail; she sewed her own embroidered robes; on Mondays, she regaled us with tales of jousting and complicated allegiances.

"I'm sorry, but that is so weird," En says.

My mother says, "So weird I can bite my toes."

"Babushka!" En yells from the back. "Why do you always say that?"

My mother says that because when I was in college, I once quoted a line from Berke Breathed's comic strip *Bloom County*, which featured a talking penguin, a precocious ten-year-old boy, a disinhibited, self-destructive defense attorney, and a scraggly orange cat. At least I think that's where the line was from–I vaguely remember joking around, saying, "I love this so much I can bite my toes" about something I didn't actually love, and my mother seized it and has never let it go.

Each one of us has so many references we don't understand. At one point, En struggles to explain what a meme is to my mother and eventually gives up. My mother and I will never be able to properly explain Russian words and concepts like *toska*, which has no single linguistic equivalent in English, and which, loosely and imperfectly translated, means yearning, sadness, longing, melancholy, though for what or whom it's impossible to say. En is mad at me because I never taught her Russian, but the reasons I never taught her Russian are untranslatable.

I'm an only child and En is the youngest and only girl in our family and my mother is Grandma Ester's only surviving child. Grandma Ester herself was the last of eight children and the only girl; Grandma Tsilya, the youngest of three sisters, two of whom perished in the war. There's a specific, peculiar kind of loneliness in that. The only, the last.

After I met my cousin Masha in 2022, we began speaking on Zoom almost weekly, for hours at a time. We recognized something about each other almost immediately–the same curiosity about language, the same reverence for books, the same expansive hand gestures, the same dark humor, the same painful self-consciousness born of being the only child subjected to the watchful gaze of immigrant parents, the same restless longing for something we couldn't name. Masha is sixteen years younger than me and sixteen years older than En, and she and En look weirdly, remarkably similar. They could be sisters. In reality, they are distant cousins–Masha's grandfather was Grandma Ester's older brother. "*Stranno meshayetsya krov*"–how curiously blood commingles–says a character in Bulgakov's novel *The Master and Margarita.*

Masha speaks clearly and cryptically at once, in a way that I imagine the prophetess Cassandra might have spoken. She told me once that she had to turn herself inside out in order to understand who she was. She was diagnosed with diabetes in high school and rebelled against the unfairness of it and then against the unfairness of organ failure and dialysis and osteomyelitis and two amputations and doctors who said they would save the knee of her right leg but didn't–"I would be running marathons if I still had that knee," she told me once. She went blind during one of her hospitalizations but later regained sight in one eye. She is one of the most whole and luminous people I know, and even En, who is cynical and mistrustful, unsarcastically calls her a sunshine person. A sunshine person is someone who makes the world brighter and warmer by being in it.

When Masha goes out, others see a woman with long dark-brown hair and piercing dark eyes on a motorized scooter. The scooter is named Penelope IV because it's the fourth iteration of the same scooter and because Penelope is loyal and clever and patient. In one of our Zoom calls, Masha told me she rarely thinks about her amputations, but she understands that they're a way for the world to read her–to understand the intensity of the internal experience that led to an outward expression of that pain. "It's language the world can process," she said, "and isn't that part of being human–wanting to be truly understood?"

In the back seat, En drops her phone, which slides under the front passenger seat. She fumbles for it, muttering, "Why is this happening to me, a mostly good person?"

"Story of my life," I say.

"So true, bestie," says En.

Mostly good people

Jane Lathrop Stanford and Leland Stanford Sr. had a son, Leland Jr., born to them after eighteen childless years. When the boy was sixteen, he died from typhoid fever, and his grieving parents founded a university in his memory. The cornerstone for Stanford University was laid on May 14, 1887, a day on which the younger Leland would have turned nineteen, had he lived.

Stanford University sits on the westernmost edge of Palo Alto. North to south, Palo Alto is bisected by a commuter rail line that runs from San Francisco through the Peninsula and Santa Clara Valley.

The train tracks for the commuter rail line were laid by the Southern Pacific Railroad, which was acquired in 1868 by the Big Four–Charles Crocker, Mark Hopkins, Collis Huntington, and Leland Stanford Sr. The Big Four got their start in Sacramento, selling hardware, iron, steel, and coal, but they quickly saw that the real money was not in the raw materials. Anyone could sell iron and coal. The real money was in converting raw materials into the very embodiment of progress–a railroad that would stretch from sea to shining sea and stitch together a country that had been torn asunder along the Mason-Dixon Line. The railroad would make the men who built it fantastically wealthy, wealthy beyond anyone's wildest dreams.

Only they didn't build it, exactly. Rather, they supervised the laying of 690 miles of Central Pacific Railroad track that would connect Sacramento to the Union Pacific Railroad tracks at Promontory Summit, Utah. The actual building–at record speed, because the essence of progress was to move fast–was done largely by Chinese laborers who sailed east from Hong Kong on overcrowded ships and then toiled in blazing hot deserts and on freezing mountain passes on land that was summarily seized from tribes that had lived on it for generations. When the Central Pacific Railroad tracks reached the Union Pacific Railroad track after six years, Leland Stanford used a silver hammer to drive in the Golden Spike during a lavish ceremony on May 10, 1869. (The spike was promptly removed to prevent theft and now sits in the Cantor Arts Center on the Stanford campus.)

People move to Palo Alto for its excellent schools and safe tree-lined streets and the scent of money and possibility that hangs in the air with the morning fog. On Waverley Street, cars slow down to photograph the house where Steve Jobs lived. Tourists stop and do a double take when they pass buildings with logos they recognize–Houzz, Flipboard–and wander down Addison Avenue looking for the garage where Bill Hewlett and Dave Packard launched HP.

West of El Camino Real, University Avenue, which runs east–west through Palo Alto, becomes a wide palm-lined boulevard that culminates in the tawny sandstone buildings of Stanford University. The fastest swimmers, the highest pole-vaulters, the most nimble tech visionaries come from Stanford. Stanford was where Eadweard Muybridge captured the surge of a galloping horse on film for the first time, where Dr. Bruce Reitz performed the first successful heart-lung transplant, where football coach Bill Walsh popularized the West Coast offense, where two graduate students developed a page-rank algorithm that became Google. Stanford was also where Professor Lewis Terman studied gifted children and concluded that exceptional intelligence must be nurtured and that children who appeared intellectually stunted should be segregated into separate classes.

Two of Palo Alto's three middle schools were named after prominent eugenicists who taught at Stanford–Lewis Terman and David Starr Jordan, the first president of Stanford University who almost certainly poisoned Jane Lathrop Stanford. The two middle schools were renamed in 2018, but legacies endure, even with new names.

Surviving children

Both Grandma Tsilya and Grandma Ester had a little boy who died during wartime, before each of my parents was born. Grandma Tsilya's son, whose name, David, I learned only recently, was born three years before my father and died of diphtheria before he turned two. Grandma Ester's son was named Valeriy.

Both of my parents grew up in the shadow of older brothers they never knew. My father is the oldest of two surviving sons; my mother, the second child and the oldest of two daughters. In a neatly symmetrical arrangement, Grandma Tsilya lived with my paternal aunt and uncle and Grandma Ester lived with my maternal aunt and uncle. Both grandmothers helped raise my younger cousins. From them I learned that children needed to be two things: successful and safe.

Money talks

I am convinced that Mike White, the creator of *The White Lotus*, has read Henry James. What else, I ask En and my mother, can explain the series' preoccupation with money and with rich, uncouth, arrogant Americans blundering through exotic locales? What is that if not James's international theme adapted for the digital age? White's vacationing Americans are a lot like James's Americans abroad–optimistic and artless and certain of their invincibility. Especially Tanya McQuoid, the fantastically wealthy, vapid heiress who makes her assistant sign a nondisclosure agreement (because money talks and penury doesn't) and asks for Oreo cake at breakfast and takes everything and everyone at face value.

We're between Santa Margarita and Atascadero when I tell En and my mother to keep an eye out for how money, language, and meaning intersect in the show. "I don't want to give anything away, but it's straight out of Henry James," I say.

In James, the value of words–just like the value of money–is determined not by their intrinsic value but by an agreed-upon system of meaning. James was a young man when the US government began issuing greenbacks–paper money–to finance the Civil War, and unlike gold and silver coins, which broadcast their value with their heft and substance, greenbacks were flimsy and insubstantial and suspect. Like words–even weighty words like *love* or *catastrophe* or *joy*–they were real only insofar as enough people agreed on their value. But in their flimsiness lay their power: They were fungible. James's Americans exchange new wealth for old status: crisp dollar bills for Italian palazzos, for marriage into ancient noble bloodlines.

I know I'm being didactic, but I can't help myself. It's been so long since I've talked about my dissertation, and here it is, suddenly relevant. (To me, at least.) My mother is nodding attentively, and En–presumably–is listening in the back seat. Either that or she has her AirPods in and she's listening to music.

"This is what I find so interesting," my mother says. "How can a country founded on the principles of equality be so preoccupied with class and breeding?"

"That's what I'd like to know," I say.

Apart from my dissertation advisors, who had to read it, the only other person who read every page of my dissertation was my mother. She also read all the books I referenced in it, including James's dense, impenetrable, brilliant last novel–*The Golden Bowl.*

"OMG, *that's* what that book was called!" En calls out. "*The Golden Bowl.* For some reason, I thought it was called *A Bowl of Soup.*"

Fungible goods

My parents and I left the Soviet Union with four suitcases. This is a central part of our family mythos. Three of the suitcases contained essentials: clothing, shoes, toiletries, a travel voltage converter, a small selection of tools, a hot plate, and an uncensored copy of Mikhail Bulgakov's *The Master and Margarita*, which my parents received as a gift from friends who lived in East Berlin and which they were technically not supposed to have. The fourth suitcase was stuffed with small, enticing luxuries I was under strict orders not to touch: lacquered Russian spoons, boxes, and nesting dolls, delicate Vologda lace, strings of coral beads, tins of black caviar, and Cuban cigars. The boxes of cigars enticed me most of all, because of the pretty picture and the gold coins on the lid and also because I was convinced that they held chocolate in spite of my parents' repeated insistence to the contrary.

The contents of the fourth suitcase were for selling at the Mercato Porta Portese, a flea market in Rome's Trastevere neighborhood. Every Sunday, newly arrived Soviet émigrés would make their pilgrimage to the market–which, for obscure reasons, everyone referred to as the Americana–to sell virtually identical caviar tins, strings of coral beads, lace, cigars, and lacquered spoons and matryoshkas in order to supplement the weekly allowance for food and rent that came from the Hebrew Immigrant Aid Society. That was how my parents managed to scrape together enough money to travel throughout Italy for almost a month.

My parents exchanged a suitcase full of caviar tins and lace and wooden tchotchkes for Italian lire, and then they exchanged the lire for train tickets and cheap hotel rooms where the three of us slept in one bed. It was late October–overcast, windy, occasionally spitting rain–which was bad, but everything was cheaper and less crowded, which was good. We visited Naples and Pompeii and Capri, where the wind blew so fiercely that my mother said later that she was convinced we were all going to die on the chairlift to Monte Solaro. Then we headed north, to the tiny country of San Marino, and then further north–to Verona, to see the very house with the very balcony depicted on the cigar boxes (I was still skeptical that the boxes contained cigars and not chocolate, but it was too late to find out, because the cigars had been converted to money that had been converted to going to Verona). In Siena, my parents fought bitterly about something neither of them remembers and my mother sat fuming on one side of the shell-shaped Piazza del Campo while my father sat fuming on the other, and I traveled between them like a small and bewildered emissary and eventually they reconciled. Then we got to Venice.

The shape of what my parents and I remember about our time in Italy is roughly the same, and when it isn't, one of us will often sketch in what's missing. But with regard to Venice, our memories differ sharply.

What my mother remembers: that Venice was more expensive than she and my father had anticipated. After booking the cheapest hotel they could find (it was cold and damp, it was getting dark, it was starting to rain, they couldn't keep looking forever), my parents discovered that they didn't have enough money left for dinner. Dinner was the same every night everywhere we went: half a rotisserie chicken. The other half was made into chicken soup on our trusty hot plate, which also boiled water for tea.

We left our suitcases at the hotel and went sightseeing, and at some point I said I was hungry and my parents tried to distract me by pointing out the canals and the buildings and the bridges, but I would not be dissuaded and repeated that I was hungry, and after no one answered I demanded to know when we were going to have chicken. There was no chicken, because there was no money.

My mother asks, "Can you imagine? Your child tells you she's hungry and you have nothing to give her?"

"Babushka, that is *so* sad," En says. "You must have felt terrible."

What's funny is that I don't remember being hungry in Venice, or anywhere else we went. I honestly don't remember what we ate in Italy–I do know we didn't go to restaurants, because occasionally we would pass a window behind which was flickering candlelight, people eating and drinking, light reflected on the curve of a wine glass, and it looked pretty but foreign, like a stage set. It was not for us. What I do remember, clearly, was waiting in the small lobby of our Venice hotel while my parents were checking out and taking out my notebook and pen so I could sketch a sculpture of a nude woman that stood on a small table near the front desk. The sculpture was made of blue glass; the woman was stepping out of a robe that flowed in a way I didn't know glass could flow. I was so absorbed in what I was doing that I didn't notice that the adults were finished with their adult business and that the woman at the front desk was standing behind me and looking over my shoulder until she said, "*Molto bene, bellissima.*" Her words made me feel shy and pleased and then something even better happened: She went back behind the counter and emerged with a tiny book of miniature fold-out postcards of Venice, which she presented to me with a flourish.

We were so preoccupied with money–how much we had, how long it would last. One of the first phrases we acquired when we came to Italy was "*Quanto costa?*"–how much? As new arrivals in Rome, we lived in a residential hotel for several days before we found a room in an apartment near the Vatican. The hotel had a coin-operated elevator, which required a fifty-lire coin, and my father drilled a small hole in the coin and threaded a string through it so we could pay using the same coin again and again. I want to say the hotel was called Olympia, because how fitting is that? But a fitting name is not always accurate, and neither one of my parents remembers what the hotel was actually called. ("Just say it was called Olympia," says David.)

The woman in the lobby of our Venice hotel waved my father off when he reached into his pocket for money he didn't have. She wanted me to have the miniature book of postcards for free, for drawing something beautiful.

Class and breeding

Here's how success worked in America: You came with nothing, you found a job, you worked hard, you bought things you couldn't have in Soviet Russia—cars, color televisions, jeans, athletic shoes, McDonald's hamburgers, houses. Your children benefited from your sacrifices and your hard work, attended excellent schools, landed lucrative jobs, married well, produced their own successful children. And so on.

In April 1987—*April is the cruelest month*—my seven-year-old cousin Benji drowned on a family vacation in Mexico. (*If you're not home, you're in danger.*) Benji was the first in our family to be born in the United States. He was precocious and funny and kind; he could have been president—he could have been anything. His loss hollowed out his parents and his older sister, undid Grandma Tsilya, and made unsteady the ground under our feet. "My father, and now . . ." my uncle Boris said after Benji's funeral. He didn't finish the sentence.

The teen suicides in Palo Alto began in 2008, or maybe in 2002. It depends on who you talk to, and most people in Palo Alto don't want to talk about it. Many of the suicides occurred on the tracks that once belonged to the railroad barons who built the first transcontinental railroad. In 2015, *The Atlantic* ran a cover story titled "The Silicon Valley Suicides: Why Are So Many Kids with Bright Prospects Killing Themselves in Palo Alto?" and in

2016, the Centers for Disease Control and Prevention launched an investigation. The CDC released its findings in 2017, recommending a "strategic, data-driven approach to suicide prevention and the use of multiple programs and strategies as part of a comprehensive and coordinated prevention approach." The report also encouraged "strategies to strengthen parent-youth relationships," which was bullshit, because everyone knew that many of those who had died were raised by well-off, loving parents who wanted nothing but the best for their children.

Labor and delivery

My mother is telling En about giving birth to me in a Soviet hospital on the same day that Russian tanks entered Prague, ostensibly to rescue their Czech brethren from the perils of capitalism but really to annex then-Czechoslovakia to the Soviet Union. "I'm having contractions and the radio is blaring, 'The Czech people are at this moment welcoming their glorious Soviet liberators,' and I wanted to throw up," she says.

I've heard my mother's story before, as well as her description of the abysmal conditions in the maternity ward and the story about the Georgian man (the man's Georgianess is an important detail as Georgian men are even more macho than Russian men) who stood under the window of the maternity ward bellowing for his wife. The nurse tried to send him away, but eventually the wife, who had just given birth, made her way to the window, and the man couldn't believe she'd had a girl, not a boy. My mother reports that he yelled, "A boy, yes?" when she appeared in the window, and after she shook her head weakly, there was a dumbfounded pause and then he yelled, "Well, what then?"

En says, "What an asshole!" and then asks me to tell the story about a dream I had when I was pregnant with Nemo. "The symbolism is so good," she tells my mother, who has not heard this story, even though it happened under her own roof.

The meaning of dreams

When I was pregnant with Nemo, David and I drove up to Sunnyvale to stay with my parents for spring break, our cat Gaby in tow. Gaby had to stay in our room because my father, like Grandma Tsilya, is not a friend of animals, and Gaby did not care for being stuck in a small room in an unfamiliar house. She expressed her displeasure by meowing all night long, and between her meowing and my unwieldy pregnant belly, it took me until early morning to fall into a fitful sleep.

In my dream, David and I were in the same bedroom as we were in real life, but instead of a cat, there was an enormous black snake writhing by the door, and the most terrifying part was that the face on the snake was Gaby's. I take it back: The slow, muscular undulations and the combination of cat and snake was the second-most terrifying part. The first was that there was a phone by our bed, and I picked up the receiver to call 911–if this wasn't an emergency I don't know what was–but instead of the 911 operator, I got my mother, who in the dream picked up an extension elsewhere in the house and somehow knew that I was calling 911. She asked me whether anything was wrong, and I said no, of course not, and hung up, and then I tried again and the same thing happened and she asked me why I was calling 911 and I said, oh, no reason, I must have misdialed by accident.

Even in the dream, it was clear what the rules were: Don't cause unnecessary worry. Keep your voice steady and pretend that everything is fine and take care of whatever needs to be taken care of on your own.

Bed and breakfast

My mother's room at the Paso Robles Marriott looks out over the freeway. En and I are across the hall, our room overlooking the parking lot. "The signora distinctly said, 'a room with a view,'" I say, doing my best imitation of Maggie Smith's plummy British accent in the movie of the same name. My mother says, "What a depressing room."

What she actually says is, "*Kakaya neuyutnaya komnata*," but *uyut*, the word at the root of *neuyutnaya*, is another Russian word that defies translation. *Uyut* means "cozy," but it contains multitudes, like the Danish word *hygge*. Not simply coziness but also contentment, comfort, conviviality.

Everyone in my family is preoccupied with living space. How much there is, how it looks, how clean it is. After my parents bought their house in Sunnyvale in the summer of 1980, Grandma Tsilya paced it out, estimating how many families it could accommodate by Soviet standards. According to her, the final tally was seven: a family in each of the three bedrooms, two families in the living room, two more in the garage.

During the wartime evacuation to Kirov, Grandma Tsilya and my infant father lived in the house of a local family that had agreed (or been forced) to take in refugees. During their first week in the house, an old woman peered at her in the hallway and said,

"Never met any Jews before." A considering pause, then a half statement, half question: "No horns." Not mean, just curious.

My mother grew up sleeping on a cot in the kitchen of a large communal apartment, where laundry boiled next to borscht, where the residents came to blows about whose turn it was to clean the bathroom. My father grew up in a single room of a three-bedroom apartment on Chicherin Street in Odesa. The room was partitioned for privacy by crisply ironed sheets hanging from the ceiling; the kitchen and the bathroom were conflict zones, and soft-spoken, tactful Grandma Tsilya was the only one who could keep the peace. One of the neighbors–a stout middle-aged woman I was under strict orders never to speak to when we visited–once threatened to chop my uncle's head off if he didn't agree to marry her daughter. Down the hall, an older couple quarreled incessantly and occasionally threw things at each other; my mother remembers meeting them soon after she and my father were married. The husband sized up my mother and said to no one in particular, "Look at her tiny hands! How will she cook with those tiny hands?"

Our Marriott rooms are comfortable and clean but far from cozy, and because it's too late to have lunch but too early to drive to the light installation, En and I sit around aimlessly and play on our phones until my mother knocks on our door and suggests we meet in her room to make a plan. En heats water for tea in the in-room espresso machine and I pull the bag of leftover croissants out of my tote. "I told you you'd thank me later!" I say triumphantly, and my mother acknowledges that she was wrong and I was right, a small concession that makes me ridiculously happy.

Over tea and croissants, we decide to head to the light installation right when it opens at 4:30 p.m. Then we'll grab a quick dinner in downtown Paso Robles and hightail it back to the Marriott to watch more *White Lotus.* Our decision is swift and unanimous. There's no stopping us. We're united by a single purpose, focused, forward-looking. If I were the kind of person who posted hashtagged pictures on Instagram, I would have taken a picture of the three of us and written "#squadgoals."

Developmental delays

The first time En demanded to know why I didn't teach her Russian, she was in middle school and Orion was in high school and Nemo had already left for college. I was making dinner; she was across the breakfast bar, pinning me with her eyes. The normally placid Orion looked up from his video game and said, "Jesus Christ, maybe Mom had other things on her mind at the time," and En told him to shut up and left the room.

Orion was right: I did have other things on my mind. After Nemo was born, I spoke to him in Russian, and my parents spoke to him in Russian, and the grandmothers spoke to him in Russian, and David and everyone else spoke to him in English, but he didn't respond in either language. When he was two, he was diagnosed with autism. Given his language delay, the diagnosing psychiatrist recommended sticking to one language. English would probably be more practical, she said.

Talk about irony (and believe me, I think about the irony all the time): While I was writing about physical and linguistic displacement in the novels of James and Nabokov, my oldest son was failing to develop meaningful language of any kind.

Accelerated curriculum

After Nemo's diagnosis, well-meaning friends sent us Emily Kingsley's poem, "Welcome to Holland." "Welcome to Holland" is about discovering that your child has special needs. Being pregnant, Kingsley writes, is like being on a plane that you think is going to Italy, but when the plane lands, the pilot says, "Welcome to Holland." You're devastated and angry because you thought you were going to be eating gelato in Piazza San Marco and tossing coins into the Trevi Fountain, and instead you're wandering in a place you never wanted to go, rageful and grief-stricken while everyone is having fun elsewhere.

The poem promises that eventually, you'll discover that Holland, too, is beautiful–windmills, tulips, wooden shoes. It's not bad, just different. You accept. You come to terms. But David and I were twenty-eight years old and frantic and terrified, and we did not want to accept or come to terms. We read every grim book about autism we could find (they were all grim, because it was 1997, and *neurodivergence* was not yet a word, but there were many other words–*disability*, *disorder*, *impairment*, *delay*) and then decided that Nemo would be the exception to the grimness. He was still so young–not even three–and he already had some words, even though our conversations went nowhere. "Do you want a waffle?" we would ask, and he would answer, "Waffle," and we would say, "Say yes," and he would say, "Yes," and then we would ask him again if he wanted a waffle and again he would answer, "Waffle." Around and around, over and over, like the wheels of the toy cars he spun close to his face.

I asked the diagnosing psychiatrist if he would ever know we were his parents, if he would ever love us, and she said it was difficult to tell, but maybe.

We decided to go with the maybe. We tried everything that had even a shred of evidence that it might help–floortime, social stories, facilitated playdates. We met with a psychodynamic child psychologist. We posted the Denver Developmental Screening Scale on our refrigerator, like a train schedule for where Nemo was supposed to be when, and we tracked his progress, counting how many words he could string together and how many wooden beads he could slide onto a string and how many body parts his stick figures had. We signed him up for occupational therapy and speech therapy; we bought a wooden puzzle called Moody Bear, which had interchangeable faces with different expressions–happy, sad, surprised, angry. We, too, were sad and surprised and angry. We envisioned worst-case scenarios–he would be bullied, he would be taken advantage of, he would never be able to live independently. It was our job to keep that from happening.

David said, "Neuroplasticity." I said, "I learned English as a second language when I was nine and I don't even have an accent." A helpful friend pointed out that Einstein didn't even speak in sentences until he was five and that before Temple Grandin became a renowned professor of animal science, she was nonverbal and threw violent tantrums and her doctors said she should be institutionalized. We would get Nemo through this, whatever "this" was.

And we did. He began to string together words and sentences and beads and added hair and eyes and arms and fingers to his stick figures. So fast, so heady was his progress that we had two more children–Orion, who was born a year after Nemo's diagnosis, and En, who was born two and a half years after Orion. We imagined a house full of laughing children, bike rides around the neighborhood, family game nights. We imagined smooth sailing. Which, of course, is not how it turned out, but you probably saw that coming a mile off.

The green world

Field of Light is a short drive from Paso Robles–through downtown, a few minutes on a one-lane highway, and then a left onto a dirt road.

Here we are, at our destination. Here it is, the whole reason the three of us have gone on this trip in the first place. The thing for which my mother and I plotted the itinerary, made reservations, texted En, blocked dates off on the calendar, braved a storm, drove hundreds of miles. Imagine the background music swelling. Imagine the symbolism: a light in the darkness, the treasure within reach.

On the drive to the light exhibit, En says, "You guys. What if it's . . . I dunno, dumb?"

I've been worrying about the same thing. But then it occurs to me that it doesn't matter whether it's dumb or not. Without noticing, we've somehow knit together, the three of us, developed a shared understanding. If it's dumb, we'll have another story to put next to the story about shrieking with gleeful terror at Ostrichland USA, about huddling together on my mother's bed at the Wine Valley Inn watching the first episode of *The White Lotus*, about our ongoing quest for baked goods and coffee with plant-based milk.

But we needn't have worried. We arrive at Field of Light right when the gates open, just as daylight begins to give way to twilight. Our timing is perfect, even though we don't yet know that twilight was the best time to come, that the air would smell clean and cold, that the sky would be bleached of all color, that the bare branches of the oak trees on the surrounding hills would edge that colorless sky like thin, uplifted arms, like lace, that an unimaginably big, unimaginably bright copper moon would be rising behind those trees–so bright that it looks like the sun. We don't yet know that the grass would be carpeted with what looks like white butterflies, or snowdrops, but are actually tens of thousands of stemmed fiber-optic spheres that drink in light from the sun all day so they can glow pink and purple and orange and blue and green at night. The darker it gets, the brighter they glow.

It's so simple–sky, grass, hills, trees, moon, lights. But the entirety of it inspires a wordless reverence, like being in a cathedral, except this is a cathedral with no walls. It's not magic–from the walking path, we can see the cables snaking among the lights–but it feels like an enchanted place. A path winds through the hills, sloping now up, now down, and as we walk it, I glimpse now my mother's face, now En's, obscured by shadow and then illuminated, like we're in the presence of something sacred, like we've wandered into a secret glade, a place in a fairy tale. I take dozens of photos and videos with my phone, even though we all agree that the real thing is so much better, that it is truly impossible to capture, in word or in image, because it's so simple, so moving, so expansive and so embracing at the same time.

Treasure

In a fairy tale, this would have been the part where the hero rescues the princess, reclaims the lost or stolen object, slays the adversary. But there's nothing to rescue or reclaim or slay at the light installation. It's simply there to look at, to walk through, to leave. I wonder briefly whether the name, Field of Light, was inspired by the Elysian Fields, a realm of the ancient Greek underworld where the virtuous and the heroic dwelt in bliss forever.

It's dark by the time we find our way to the car. The three of us are uncharacteristically quiet, and when we do speak, our voices are hushed. We're reluctant to break the spell. We don't want to forget what we've just seen. Except for several food trucks at the entrance, there are no concession stands, and even if there were, what souvenir could possibly capture the elemental beauty of the installation?

The word *souvenir* is French for "to remember." *Sou*, under, and *venir*, to come. Literally something that comes from below. When we moved to Sunnyvale, my mother wanted to throw away the four beat-up suitcases that traveled to America with us; she didn't understand why my father wanted to keep old dusty junk in the garage. I protested and said we needed to keep at least one of the suitcases, for sentimental value. The suitcase was made of pressed cardboard and covered with peeling brown paint; near the handle was a sticker bearing our Russian last name transliterated in English, strange and familiar at the same time.

Over the years, I filled the suitcase with stuffed animals I no longer slept with, letters and birthday cards, empty lipstick tubes and depleted lighters, tickets to concerts and plays, programs from high school theater productions, dried flowers, notes I passed in class, a large drawstring bag Grandma Tsilya sewed for the balalaika I was responsible for carrying when we left. The bag was made from an aggressively ugly fabric–overlapping rectangles of lizard-green, bright yellow, and orange, all scored with brown lines–but like everything else Grandma Tsilya sewed, the craftsmanship was impeccable. The contents of the suitcase are listed in a poem I wrote in my senior year; it was called "a messiah of things" (I refused to use capitals until my freshman year of college) and began with the line "i have saved everything."

Mergers and acquisitions

During our first year in San Francisco, my parents and I discovered the mind-boggling American practice of setting possessions out on a driveway and charging next to nothing for them, which is how we found a brown Formica table and four dining room chairs upholstered in turquoise vinyl for twenty dollars, as well as a nearly complete set of children's Golden Book encyclopedias. After we moved to Sunnyvale, my father continued to haunt garage sales, hauling back (among many, many other finds) several paintings, an air compressor, and an electric typewriter with a hypersensitive "l" key that fired off a row of "l's" like a machine gun if you touched it the wrong way.

There was so much to acquire. Clothes and furniture and pots and pans and cups and plates and silverware and pictures for the walls. A macramé plant hanger to hang between the dining room and the living room. The Golden Book encyclopedias from the garage sale were supposed to help me acquire English. My father handed me one of the encyclopedia volumes and an English–Russian dictionary and told me to start reading.

I did not want to start reading, but I was a dutiful Soviet child, and I complied. I saw immediately that the volume my father handed me had too many words and not enough pictures. I had to look up every single word except *the*, *a*, and *and*, and as a result of this exercise I learned exactly one word, which I still remember, but only because I stared at it for so long and with such murderous hatred. The word was *important.*

But then I discovered television, which had a better word-to-picture ratio, and the words started coming. A trickle first, then a flood. I watched *Gilligan's Island* and learned about lagoons and coconuts and castaways and movie stars and millionaires. *The Brady Bunch* taught me about blended families and pork chops and applesauce and the dangers of picking up native ceremonial objects in Hawaii. *The Beverly Hillbillies* taught me that people from Appalachia were poor and talked funny but were also honest and honorable, and *Three's Company* taught me that blondes had more fun (in sixth grade, I had a sideways ponytail just like Chrissy Snow, but I did not have more fun, which must have been because I had brown hair). And from *Laverne & Shirley* I learned that even if you didn't go to college and lived in a basement and worked in a brewery, you could still have a fun life as long as you were with your best friend. My parents hated *Laverne & Shirley* almost as much as I hated reading the Golden Book encyclopedias with an English–Russian dictionary.

The more words I acquired, the more at home I felt in my own skin–less clumsy, less lost. I collected quotes from books and poems. My parents bought books by American authors and books by Russian authors that had been banned in the Soviet Union. My father steadily added new tools to the growing collection in our garage; my mother added new creams and potions to her bathroom vanity, delighting in the cosmetic bags filled with miniature samples that came as a gift with purchase. Grandma Ester steadily collected shoes and bought inspirational plaques and tea cozies at the flea market and Ross Dress for Less and swept packets of Splenda into her purse at restaurants; Aunt Klara, who arrived in San Francisco with Uncle Isaak three years after we did, followed other shoppers around the supermarket and added whatever they were buying to her own cart if it looked intriguing.

(This explained the kiwi in the salad and other unusual, invariably delicious, dishes she served when we came over. American abundance by way of Russian favorites.)

Only Grandma Tsilya remained a minimalist. She shopped only for food or, occasionally, for fabric or sewing notions. She dressed simply; she eschewed jewelry. In the pantheon of our family, she was Hestia, the minor, unassuming goddess who watches over hearth and home, over meals, over the things that sustain us.

The things that sustain us

On our way to dinner, my mother, En, and I stop in a shop that sells scented candles and dainty gold earrings and expensive throw pillows and small ceramic bowls, and I buy two bars of artisanal chocolate–one for my father, one for David–and a bottle of locally made hot sauce for Orion, because he likes to put hot sauce on everything, the hotter the better.

Orion lives at home and works full-time at a store that sells, in his words, bougie athleisure wear. As a result, he has upgraded his wardrobe and become an expert on sustainable fabrics and recent trends in hoodies and joggers. I don't buy anything for Nemo, because he lives in San Diego, where he teaches physical education at an elementary school.

At various junctures, each one of our children has moved back home, mostly out of necessity. En couldn't wait to leave. Neither could Nemo. Orion is the only one who seems content living at home. He has his routines, his comforts, a repertoire of terrible puns that make David and me laugh. He does not share his siblings' intense dislike of Palo Alto.

The problem with Palo Alto

The problem with Palo Alto is what enticed me and David to move to Palo Alto in the first place. The world-class university practically in our backyard, the sought-after schools, the high expectations. All good things, until they weren't.

It's possible that I was part of the problem. After receiving my PhD and working for several years as a humanities lecturer, I began working in the Stanford admissions office. Working in the admissions office made me valuable in a way that writing about exile and meaning-making in the lives and works of James and Nabokov never could. It gave me secret, coveted knowledge, and when I opened my own college counseling practice, the money poured in.

For many years, David and I shared an office in an imposing three-story office building in downtown Palo Alto. Five-fifty Hamilton Avenue was built in the early 1970s but styled to look much older, sort of like a Spanish hacienda. A large oil painting of rolling fields and trees–depicting, presumably, what Silicon Valley looked like before it became Silicon Valley–hung on the landing between the first and second floors. The building was occupied by mental health professionals, venture capitalists, and small start-ups. I should probably mention here that David is a psychiatrist.

There was a lot of money in that building. There was also a lot of anguish. Hardworking and anxious parents and hardworking anxious students, all of them convinced that no matter how hard they worked, or how many Advanced Placement courses they took, it was not enough. It was never enough. Enough for what? For Stanford, mostly, but also for other "good" schools, "good" meaning almost impossible to get into. My job was to help the families I worked with navigate the college application process, sort of like Virgil guiding Dante through the ten circles of hell, but with SAT scores. David's job was to help his patients manage their depression and anxiety, which was often but not always connected to the pressures of living in Palo Alto. The irony of that juxtaposition is not lost on me.

I want to be clear: Neither David nor I had any interest in grooming our children to be candidates to "good" colleges. We did not buy Stanford swag or enroll them in summer enrichment courses that would result in accelerated class placement in the fall. But we lived in a place where that was the norm, where the unofficial motto was "Move fast and break things." We didn't want to break things, but we also didn't want to get left behind. We wanted our children to live up to their full potential. We did not realize that their full potential was not for us to decide.

Rota Fortunae

The Greek goddess Tyche, whose domains were fate, providence, luck, and chance, was often depicted with a rudder, guiding and conducting the affairs of the world, or a ball, which could roll in any direction, or a cornucopia, signifying plenty. The Romans renamed her Fortuna and endowed her with a spinning wheel.

That's just how life was: You were at the top of the world, and then you weren't. Maybe you risked everything to come to a new country and you hit the jackpot. Maybe you got pregnant on the first try and then your child was diagnosed with a serious developmental disorder, and then you had two more children in quick succession without thinking through all the things that could go wrong, and there were so many things that could go wrong, and did go wrong, and when you tried to fix them you made them worse. Or maybe the tuberculosis you had in your twenties returned and killed you before your fortieth birthday, as it killed Ilya Ilf shortly after he and Evgeniy Petrov finished writing *Roadside America* in 1938. Or maybe, like Evgeniy Petrov, the airplane you were flying in was downed by German fire as you were returning from a reporting assignment in 1942. Or maybe you just got on the wrong airplane.

Fear of flying

It's Friday evening, and unlike Solvang, downtown Paso Robles is packed. We didn't think we'd need restaurant reservations–perhaps we didn't think we'd make it this far in our trip–but now every restaurant has a long wait. Just as we're about to begin bickering, En spots a Mexican restaurant and the hostess tells us she can seat us right now if we can be out in an hour. We tell her yes, easily, we have somewhere to be right after. We follow her to our table and give each other significant looks, because where we have to be is in my mother's hotel room, bingeing *The White Lotus.*

Over chips and salsa, we discuss the looming end of our trip, how fast it went, how much we managed to cram into just a day and a half, much of it serendipitous. Our conversation turns to travel, and En says she wants to go back to New Zealand and Australia but adds that being cooped up in an airplane for such a long time is crazy-making. My mother sighs and says she loves to travel but that flying is the worst part. She has been a nervous flier her entire life. She tells us that my grandfather once said something she tries to remember every time her plane is about to take off: Just think of all the engineers and scientists who built this plane, all the knowledge and ingenuity it took to get it into the air. The marvel of it.

The first time I heard these words from my mother was in my sophomore year of college. Eight months after my cousin Benji drowned, a Pacific Southwest Airlines flight from LA crashed en route to San Francisco because a disgruntled employee on board shot and killed the flight crew. My usually stoic mother called me, sobbing. "It could have been you on that plane," she said through her tears, and suddenly I could imagine it all: the uncontrolled descent, the screaming passengers, the fiery moment of impact, oblivion. She was not normally given to weeping, at least not publicly. Her tears had to mean something. Maybe she knew or felt something I didn't.

Three months after the PSA crash, I had to fly home for my cousin Vicki's bat mitzvah and the thoughts wouldn't stop: What if my flight home was doomed? Maybe it would be better to switch flights–but what if I was wrong? What if the flight I switched to crashed instead? All those passengers on the flight that crashed had gotten on the plane thinking everything would be fine, stowed their luggage in the overhead bins, watched the safety presentation, asked the flight attendant for a ginger ale, a Diet Coke, a coffee. I became obsessed with somehow figuring out a way to know in advance, a way to not get on the wrong plane.

My fear of flying metastasized into a fear of death: What if someone forced me into a passing car as I walked to class? What if I was caught in the crossfire of a shooting? I began carrying a pair of manicure scissors in the outside pocket of my backpack so I could fight back against a possible abductor. I couldn't understand why no one else could see it, this yawning abyss right under our feet, the skull grinning just beneath the skin. When I read *Tess of the d'Urbervilles* in a Victorian literature seminar and came to the passage where it occurs to Tess that somewhere on the calendar lay the day of her death, "a day sly and unseen among all the other days of the year, giving no sign or sound," I shook with recognition. Tess understood, and I understood, and the obliviously happy people around me were idiots.

A week before Vicki's bat mitzvah, I called my parents and said that I was thinking of going to student psych services because I couldn't stop thinking about death and dying. My father said that we all come into the world by accident and that we were likely to leave it by accident and since there was nothing any of us could do about it, I might as well try to live a meaningful life. My mother said to pull myself together and stop with the nonsense. I told her that I might not fly home for Vicki's bat mitzvah because I was afraid that my plane would crash. My mother said that Vicki and her parents were still grieving and that this was no time for melodrama. Then she told me what my grandfather told her–think of the scientists, the engineers, the marvel of knowledge and shared effort it takes to get a plane in the air. But I was unconvinced, and she must have sensed my skepticism, because she ended our conversation with the Russian equivalent of "You'll get your butt on that plane and come to the bat mitzvah."

I got my butt on the plane and it didn't crash and my fear receded but it did not disappear.

Valor

When my mother first learned to drive, Grandma Ester sat in the front and comprehensively cursed out any car within a quarter-mile radius, including those that honked when my mother turned the wrong way onto a one-way street. "Stop honking, morons!" she shouted in Russian, shaking her fist as my trembling mother backed up the way she came.

I always felt safer with Grandma Ester when I drove. She would yell, "Where do you think you're going, you old fart?" at a mild-looking middle-aged man trying to pull out of a parking lot, or "You piece of shit, don't drive so close to my granddaughter!" at a woman in a station wagon two lanes over. Fortunately the other drivers couldn't understand her Russian, and her belligerence made me laugh, and it was deeply comforting to know that someone in the car thought I could do no wrong, because I was the future.

Foretelling the future

We watch four episodes of *The White Lotus*, one right after the other, as soon as we return from dinner: "Italian Dream," "Bull Elephants," "In the Sandbox," and "That's Amore." As the credits are rolling on "In the Sandbox," I look at my watch and note that it's long past midnight, but En says, "We're bingeing!" with great glee, and my mother asks, "Maybe just one more?"

En shouts, "Babushka! Hell yeah!" and reaches her hand up for a high five, and my mother high-fives her, and I press "play" again.

Apart from brief bathroom breaks, we hit pause only once: when Tanya, distraught after her husband leaves Taormina under a flimsy pretext, consults an old Sicilian fortune teller. The fortune teller lays out a spread of tarot cards in Tanya's sumptuous suite and informs her that her husband is in love with someone beautiful. "Well, that'd be me," says Tanya. "No," says the fortune teller flatly, "not you."

"Wait wait wait," En says urgently, and reaches out to pause the video. "I need to see the cards."

Portents and prophecies

En is fascinated by tarot. "I'm not woo-woo or anything," she says when my mother and I ask her about it, even though we haven't said that she was. She hugs her knees to her chest and tells us how when she was in the South Pacific, she and Ellie and two other girls bought a tarot card deck in a bookshop in New Zealand and did readings for each other. The readings were scarily accurate. "They end up coming true, just not necessarily in ways you expect," she says.

En is drawn to tarot's evocative, elemental images–the chariot, the wheel of fortune, the moon, the devil, the fool. They offer a framework for interpreting the world, just as bird signs offered the ancient Greeks a framework for interpreting the world. A pregnant hare torn apart by two eagles foretold the sacrifice of Iphigenia at Aulis; Penelope's dream of an eagle killing a goose augurs Odysseus's return to Ithaca and the slaughter of the suitors.

En has vivid, surreal dreams, which she regularly recounts in detail. Sometimes she doesn't remember the details, just the visceral, consuming terror. Sometimes she gives her dreams titles that sound like poem fragments–the frogs of April, the ghosts of Oklahoma. She dreams of being chased, running down hallways, frantic movement. She once dreamt about being at my parents' apartment and getting sent on an errand by my mother. In the dream, my mother handed her the keys to her car, whose name–and En swears this is true–was Garbaggio, and told her that Garbaggio's steering was pretty messed up and the brakes didn't really work, but that it would probably be okay. "So I just went barreling down the street, and there were all these old people around, and I was just trying to avoid hitting them, and then I woke up because I was panicking," she says.

The symbolism is so good

An out-of-control car with faulty steering and no brakes to speak of. A circuitous ten-year voyage that could have been so much less circuitous, so much shorter. A ship of fools, with an earnest, well-intentioned crew constantly working at cross-purposes.

After Odysseus and his crew escape the enraged Cyclops, they come to an island ruled by Aeolus, the god of winds, who welcomes them with food and wine and luxurious accommodations. Aeolus is eager to hear the tale of the Trojan War, and Odysseus and his men are eager to tell it and grateful for the respite. So pleased is Aeolus with their storytelling that on their departure, he supplies them with provisions and throws in a mighty bag in which he has trapped all the winds except for a gentle homeward breeze. Aeolus instructs Odysseus not to open the bag under any circumstances, but Odysseus dozes off after they set sail and his men, believing that the bag contains treasure, open it. In the ensuing gale, their ship is driven off course and back to Aeolus's island. Aeolus, furious and convinced that Odysseus is cursed, refuses to provide any further help and sends them away.

Curses

For a long time, I blamed Palo Alto for everything. It was like the sorceress Circe–beautiful and dangerous. It lured us in and turned us into swine. To live in Palo Alto was to live in a state of anxious insufficiency, because there was always more to want–more stock options, a bigger house, a nicer car, the best colleges, the shiniest trophies, the most Advanced Placement classes, the most accomplished children. It made me think of Tantalus in Hades, always hungry, always thirsty, food and water forever out of his reach. "Stay hungry, stay foolish," Steve Jobs said in his address to the Stanford graduating class of 2005.

The curse of the House of Atreus started with Tantalus, who invited the Olympian gods to a feast, butchered his own son, and served the pieces (presumably under a heavy sprinkling of parsley) to test the gods' omniscience. The gods recognized the profanation at once–all except for Demeter. Demeter, distracted by grief for her abducted daughter, Persephone, absent-mindedly nibbled on Pelops's shoulder blade, and after the gods cast Tantalus down to Hades to be eternally tormented by hunger and thirst, they reassembled Pelops and replaced his shoulder blade with an ivory one. We may have forgotten these stories, but they undergird our culture–internecine violence, lost children, insatiable desires, inconsolable grief, inexorable fate. Persephone and Pelops and Iphigenia and Telemachus, searching for his lost father, and the baby Astyanax, son of Hector, flung to his death from the Trojan walls.

Was it Tantalus's fault that generations later Agamemnon sacrificed his daughter? Was it my parents' fault that our children were struggling, because without the extra money we would have lived a simpler, better life elsewhere? (Would we have, though? The grass is always greener wherever we're not.) Was it David's and my fault, because we rushed ahead when we should have proceeded with caution? Or–and this should have been a comforting thought, but it wasn't–maybe it was no one's fault at all, maybe this was all supposed to happen, but what were we supposed to do with *that*?

Go to sleep

Even though it's almost 2 a.m., En and I are still buzzing. We've seen so much in one day–the ostriches, the lights, four back-to-back episodes of *The White Lotus*. *The White Lotus* especially gives us no peace, even though I've already seen it once, because En's enthusiasm is contagious. She's fascinated by how each character's actions are catching up with them, and not just their actions, but who they are at their core. The proverbial chickens are coming home to roost, and En is here for all of it. She has questions, even though she knows I'm not going to answer any of them, and comments, which I'm more than happy to engage with. We're both impressed by the deft way Mia sidelines the regular hotel singer and takes his place; we agree that Cameron, the finance bro, is becoming more insufferable by the minute, and that Daphne, his sunny, seemingly shallow wife, possesses unexpected depths. And the palazzo where Tanya sees two men having sex 100 percent has sinister vibes, especially at night, especially with the ominous, shifting shadows, the low, flickering, deceptive lights.

"On that note, we should get some sleep," I say from my side of the room, and En reluctantly agrees, but I can hear her tossing and turning for a long time, and it's well after 2 a.m. when we finally drift off.

We are such stuff / As dreams are made on

The first time I read *The Tempest*, I was a junior in college and David and I were a year away from getting engaged and I was entranced by the romance between Miranda and Ferdinand and equally entranced by Prospero's immense, moody power. Every word that left his mouth was so soaring, so gorgeously lyrical, so valedictory, that I would pause while reading and whisper lines to myself: "We are such stuff / As dreams are made on, and our little life / Is rounded with a sleep."

Prospero–formerly Duke of Milan, avid reader, self-taught sorcerer–is placed in a leaky boat with his infant daughter and his beloved books and exiled. That's it–a baby girl and books, which he uses to teach himself sorcery. That's all he needs. Nothing else matters anyway, because ultimately, everything dissolves into thin air–the cloud-capped towers, the palaces, the temples, the great globe itself.

I wanted to be like that, concerned only with beauty and wisdom and justice. But I inherited Grandma Ester's acquisitiveness, and I coveted *things*–rings and dangly earrings and scarves, which I rarely wore but couldn't resist because their colors and patterns spoke to me (*like this, you do not have*), and blank notebooks that I started but hardly ever filled. Attractive serving platters. Thrifted cocktail glasses with gold rims. Tube after tube of lipstick that promised the perfect red lip and ended up turning my lips a tawdry fuchsia.

Also, we had children, and our house was full of toys and swim goggles and shin guards and homework folders and screechy violin music. On top of that, I started running–first to lose weight after giving birth to three children in six years, then to escape the chaos at home, eventually to train for a marathon–and there was running gear. Shoes, a belt that held a water bottle and energy supplements for long runs, leggings, tank tops, moleskin for blisters, an iPod shuffle because I couldn't bear the sound of my own labored breathing and I didn't want to be alone with my thoughts. My power song was Bonnie Tyler's "Holding Out for a Hero," although I was also partial to Gloria Gaynor's "I Will Survive" and will.i.am's version of "I Like to Move It."

Decluttering

I didn't realize just how much stuff we had until it was time to move out of our house and into a rental because by the fall of 2007, David and I had finally saved enough money to begin remodeling our house.

Our remodel was set to begin on a Thursday in September 2007, which happened to be the same day we were scheduled to move into a rental house just a block away. (What luck, to have found something so close!) It so happened that my twenty-mile training run for the October marathon was scheduled for the following day, which I didn't know when I made arrangements with the movers, and which I wasn't going to change because it would throw off the entire training schedule. It so happened that the subprime mortgage crisis was already in full swing, and people were being evicted from homes they could no longer afford, and so I was riven with guilt about remodeling while other people no longer had homes.

The demolition crew showed up earlier than expected, and I discovered that I hadn't cleared out several upper cabinets in the kitchen, and the workmen were splintering walls with sledgehammers while I threw jars of paprika and allspice and boxes of Cheerios and rolls of paper towels into black Hefty trash bags. ("Ah, poor man's Samsonite!" a neighbor joked when he saw me dragging them onto the driveway, and I said, "Ha ha" although I really wanted to say something so vicious that it would turn him to stone.) David had already left for work; I rushed the kids to school and came back to discover that we had also forgotten to clean out an improvised loft in our garage. Right then the movers showed up and wanted to know where to start. I had no idea where to start, and one of the demo guys asked if I wanted help taking all the stuff down from the loft, and I said yes, please. I couldn't even remember what was up there.

What was up there were dusty toys, ride-on push cars, an old comforter, a fake houseplant, a slow cooker, an oversized pasta pot, a bread machine David and I bought years earlier in a fit of misplaced optimism, a stroller we meant to give away but hadn't, winter jackets we had never used because it was too difficult to take our children anywhere but family camp for the one sacred week each summer, and a large white oblong box. So many things. It made me dizzy to look at them, so I left them on the side of our driveway and told the demolition crew I'd be back in an hour because I needed to follow the movers to our rental.

It so happened that the movers dropped a file cabinet in which David kept his patient files when they were unloading the truck in front of our rental house, and two of the drawers flew open and disgorged files everywhere–dozens and dozens of manila folders and hundreds of pages of patient notes in David's small, economical handwriting, flapping in the street like so many wounded birds. I scrambled to gather them up, and the foreman jumped off the back of the truck and said, "Oh shit. Oh shit, isn't your husband a shrink?" and I said yes, he was, and then the foreman yelled at the guy who dropped the file cabinet to move his ass and help pick up the fucking papers, and the three of us reassembled them as best we could, and after the beds and the books and the boxes of kitchen stuff were unloaded, I drove back to our house.

The entire time, I was carrying a plastic laundry basket with the essentials for my run the following day: leggings, a sports bra, a T-shirt, socks, running shoes, packets of GU, a belt with an attached water bottle. The basket was my anchor. It was also my life preserver, because without it I would drown. And when I pulled into our driveway and saw the pile of toys and jackets and bedding and appliances we never used and the large white oblong box, I truly felt like I was going under. I had forty minutes before it was time to pick En up from school, so I had to make some quick decisions about what to keep and what to take to Goodwill.

It so happened that the white oblong box contained my wedding dress, which I realized when I picked it up and saw a glimpse of ivory silk through the plastic window. It had been meticulously cleaned and preserved, cocooned in layers of tissue paper and nestled in a sealed box the shape and size of a coffin. The box had been in my parents' custody since our wedding until we moved to Palo Alto, into a house that was finally big enough to store a box containing a wedding dress.

I stared at the box, and I suddenly hated the dress, hated it passionately–how big and gaudy and cumbersome it was, how young and unencumbered I was when I wore it. How the day after the wedding, David and I drove down to LA to start medical school and graduate school with all our worldly goods in the trunk of a two-door Toyota Celica. How it wasn't even the dress I wanted, and now it was an albatross I would have to carry with me, from our house to the rental and back again, so that years from now I could hand it to En and it would become her burden. Wasn't she already carrying enough? What if she didn't want it? What if it didn't fit her? Why should the dress molder in a box for years when someone else could be wearing it right now? I knew how much the dress meant to my mother–she and my father were married by a clerk at ZAGS, the government registry office, after waiting in line with hundreds of other couples in a procedure utterly devoid of ceremony or formality–but at that moment, I wanted nothing more than to never see it again.

It so happened that there was a box cutter in my jeans pocket, and I slashed the box open without thinking, and then I drew back because it felt like an act of savagery, a desecration. In the hot afternoon sun, the dress glared a blinding white. Did Iphigenia wear white? I was not thinking clearly. I was not in my right mind. The laundry hamper with my running tights and my Asics and my packets of GU sat on the driveway behind me. It was getting late and I didn't have time to waste, and anyway, I had already opened the box and so I picked up the wedding dress–the bodice pliant and limp, like a newly dead body, the full skirt stiff and unwieldy–and shoved it into the minivan, on top of the ride-on push cars and the pasta pot and the bread machine and the slow cooker and the toys and the jackets, and then I drove to Goodwill.

I don't want to imagine my mother's face when she finds out that I've given the dress away. I tell myself that I'm shielding her–or maybe it's myself I'm trying to shield. There is only so much I can hold.

Part 3

OBJECTS IN REAR VIEW

January 7: Paso Robles–Palo Alto

"I am private; you are guarded; she will steal anyone's story, throw anyone to the sharks for the sake of a book."

–Elizabeth McCracken, *The Hero of This Book*

"Then practice losing farther, losing faster: places, and names, and where it was you meant to travel."

–Elizabeth Bishop, "One Art"

Carousel

Whenever we travel with checked luggage, I stand anxiously by the carousel and watch the delivery chute. All those lives, disgorged onto the circling belt. Hard-shelled valises in bright colors and sausage-shaped duffel bags and mysterious black containers–musical instruments? construction equipment?–and trunks and strollers and heavily taped cardboard boxes and nondescript suitcases thudding and thudding, circling and circling.

When En left for her gap year in the South Pacific, I tied a red ribbon to the zipper of her duffel bag so she could easily find it in the chaos of baggage claim. So many passengers, craning their necks eagerly, reaching for any bag that looks familiar. What if someone were to walk away with hers?

Private property

Because no one lives in a vacuum, my story is not only my story. It's tangled with other stories, stories that may or may not belong to me, stories that may or may not be mine to tell.

A memoir is like a web, or a snarl, or–bear with me while I indulge in some hyperbole–a placenta. Meaty, bloody, veined. If it tears from the uterus prematurely, mother and baby die. If it comes out too late, the mother dies. It has to come out, but only at the right time. When is the right time? I have no idea, even though this is not my first memoir. All I know is that the gestation period for a human baby is nine months and the gestation period for my first memoir was twenty-five years, give or take.

My first memoir was not yet published at the time of the road trip. It had been written, and proofread, and laid out, and sent to the printer, and it would be out in the world in three months' time, and I was alternately giddy and terrified. Terrified, mostly, if I'm being honest. But it was too late to turn back.

Let's fun

En and I are bleary-eyed and slow-moving on the last morning of our trip, and so is my mother, but we decide to walk to downtown Paso Robles for coffee on the last morning of our trip. Or rather, my mother and I decide; En suggests we drive. But my mother and I persist. "It's only a mile," we say. "Some exercise before three hours in the car! It'll help us wake up!" And then my mother smiles impishly and says, "Let's fun!" and En relents.

"Let's fun" is what Lucia says in the third episode of *The White Lotus*. She and Mia are at the hotel bar, flirting with Ethan and Cameron, the two American men whose wives are spending the night in Noto. There will be a bacchanal–drinking, dancing, drugs, debauchery. Bad decisions will be made, decisions with far-ranging consequences.

Far-ranging consequences

Originally, my first memoir was going to be about how my husband David and I won our war on autism and saved our oldest son, about how brave we were, and how determined, but the story kept twisting, first one way, then another, and it was impossible to tell what, exactly, we would win when we won–or how we would even know when to claim victory. Plus, there were distractions: I worked, I did laundry, I drove carpool, I ran the elementary school book fair, I wiped down the kitchen counter. There was little time to write, and anyway, I wasn't sure what to write anymore. It had been so clear, and then it wasn't. I lost the true path and found myself in a dark wood, metaphorically speaking. Me and Dante Alighieri, who was exiled from his beloved Florence, whose *Inferno* I used to teach in Intro to Humanities when I was in graduate school, footloose and fancy-free.

Much later, I decided I would write about working as a college admissions counselor and how superior I was to the parents of the students I worked with, parents who cared only about whether their child was accepted to a prestigious college whereas I had *real* problems–an older child who struggled with a developmental disorder and his two younger siblings who struggled with growing up in Palo Alto, in a house where there was a lot of yelling because their parents were waging a war on autism while working and trying to raise three children and project competence and normalcy. And then 2020 came–terror and tedium and time to think. I went on socially distanced walks around the neighborhood with my friend Tracy, always the same route, starting and ending in the same place, day after day, and at home, I met with students on Zoom and answered the same questions about how to get into "really good schools," day after day. I thought the same thoughts, over and over: that the story was not just about my oldest son but about all of us, that perhaps Orion and En were, at least in part, casualties of our war on autism, that perhaps David and I were not that different from the parents of the students I worked with, that their desperation to ensure the best outcome for their children was the same as our desperation to ensure the best outcome for *our* children. That doing the best you could with what you knew sometimes produced devastating consequences. The road to hell being paved with good intentions and all.

It turned out I was writing a story not of *kleos* but of *nostos*–a terrible arrival at a terrible home truth. I had believed that living in the right home in the right place and doing the right things would lead to the right outcomes, and now that I found out this was not the case, I wanted to shout that truth to the world. Or at least to whoever read the memoir when it came out.

The ancient Greeks believed that erratic behavior in women was caused by the uterus wandering around inside the body; the word *hysterical* comes to us from *hystera*, the Greek word for uterus. A woman with a wandering uterus was wayward, transgressive, outlandish, unquiet, unseemly.

Perhaps I was such a woman. Erratic. Hysterical. Couldn't keep my mouth shut. Except that if I did keep my mouth shut, I would burst, or else be consumed. Grandma Ester used to shrug and say, "*Yazyk moy, vrag moy*"–my tongue is my enemy. Maybe I'm more like her than I want to admit. I can't stop talking about myself, and I drag other people into my stories, and even though everyone I wrote about in my first memoir agreed to be written about, it's one thing to agree to something in theory and another thing entirely to know that strangers have held, will hold, your story in their hands.

I made the deliberate calculation that publishing my first memoir may or may not destroy my family but continuing to live in silence and shame certainly would. We were unraveling. *Unraveling* was the word I used in my note to the cover designer. The original version of the cover had three college pennants in primary colors, one for each word of the title: *The Golden Ticket.* Yale blue for "the," yellow for "golden," Stanford red for "ticket." That was because my work as a private college admissions counselor would presumably interest parents of high schoolers, but the book wasn't just about college admissions. The book *was* an admission: Our family was floundering in Palo Alto, struggling to stay above water while we all pretended that everything was fine. There's even a name for what we were doing: *duck syndrome*, a term often applied to local high school and college students. It refers to paddling frantically underwater while presenting the illusion of gliding effortlessly on the surface. It was only a matter of time before we would be pulled under. We were drowning. I didn't want us to drown.

I apologize for the mixed metaphor. I know that unraveling isn't the same as drowning, but both were true. We were not doing well, is what I'm trying to say.

I wrote to the cover designer to say that the original design was too cheerful, that it needed to be moodier, darker somehow, that one of the pennants could be frayed, maybe? Because while I was helping tightly wound students and their families gain admission to the most coveted colleges and universities in the world, my own children were unraveling. The families I worked with were unraveling too, just in different ways. Sleep-deprived students full of self-doubt, parents anguished over the possibility that their child might not get into the right schools, worrying that they hadn't done enough, or that they had done too much, or that whatever they did wasn't good enough.

In the final design, the yellow pennant is unraveling on both ends, the loose threads barely perceptible, but there if you look closely.

I suspect Grandma Tsilya would not have approved of the memoir. *How could you*, she might have said. She would certainly not have approved of the loose threads.

In pursuit of perfection

En makes her displeasure felt as soon as my mother and I won't commit to the first coffee shop we come to. By the time we reject the third–something about lackluster pastries, something about an unwelcoming-looking barista–she exhales loudly and asks if we could just go back to the first one and stop wandering aimlessly around Paso Robles. But I want the last morning of our road trip to be perfect, and none of the coffee shops are perfect, and then I remember that my friend Debbie told me about this really good coffee place she had been to. I hadn't written down the details, because I was confident I would retain them, but now the only thing I remember is that the coffee place was really good and located in a super cute mini-mall of some sort. An outdoor marketplace maybe? I search my phone while En exhales again and then I find it and it actually does look good and meets all our requirements–plenty of seating, intricate latte art, mouthwatering pastries. It's half a mile away from where we are. Just a teeny-tiny half a mile, I say. En rolls her eyes and says, "Half a mile in the wrong direction, but *whatever*," and my mother ignores the eye roll and claps her hands and says, "Let's go," and so we do.

En used to love walking when she was little. We'd bring a stroller, and she'd shriek to be let out. She once insisted on walking the entire way to a playground almost three miles from my parents' apartment in San Francisco while I pushed her empty stroller and my parents marveled at her stamina and her older brothers complained about the hills and the distance. "Shame on you," my mother had said to them, "just look at your little sister," and En smiled a small, sly smile and went charging ahead, all pluck and determination.

Tally if you H8 Paly

Whenever the name of her high school comes up, En says #triggered, partly joking and partly not.

Palo Alto Senior High School, known familiarly as Paly, sits on the corner of El Camino Real and Embarcadero Road, across El Camino from Stanford University and across Embarcadero from a high-end open-air shopping center. It has launched a long list of celebrated industrialists, athletes, scholars, artists, and politicians. Some of them went to college across the street and some have streets named after them. Palo Alto High School is ranked ninth out of 9,006 public high schools in California. It is, by all measures, a Good School. Better than Homestead High School, which is currently ranked thirty-eighth in California. I don't know what Homestead was ranked when I went there because no one cared.

The train tracks that once belonged to the Southern Pacific Railroad run right behind Palo Alto High School. Tracks run through the school too—honors classes that branch into Advanced Placement classes. Paly students often take summer intensives—a year's worth of geometry in five weeks, for instance—so they can jump onto the faster track, the one that culminates in Advanced Placement Calculus, or maybe, if all goes well, Multivariable Calculus, which is what you take through the local community college when you exceed the available math curriculum at Paly.

For reasons too numerous and too onerous to mention, Paly was not a good school for En. She had been an early talker as a baby; she learned to read early; she astonished her elementary and middle school teachers with her quick thinking. She was all pluck, curiosity, determination, sure-footedness. And then she was diagnosed with ADHD, and suddenly she was unsure, and her timing was always off, and classes were moving too slowly or too fast, but never at the right speed. David and I tried to help, but our helping made things worse.

Toward the end of her freshman year, we suggested she consider other schools, but she refused to even look at them. She seemed resigned, like Iphigenia on the altar. "I've already started, I might as well finish," she said, and so she was miserable, and David and I were miserable. She took Adderall for ADHD and doxycycline for acne but neither one seemed to be helping, and one morning I heard her muttering to herself matter-of-factly as she was getting ready, "One pill so I'm not stupid, one pill so I'm not ugly," and I thought, *We can't live like this.* But I didn't know how, exactly, we were supposed to live.

We fielded automated calls from the attendance office letting us know that En was absent from first period (almost always, because getting out of bed was an ordeal) and sometimes from second period, and occasionally from third. The automated calls went to my cell phone and David's cell phone and our home phone and there were days when it seemed like the ringing would never stop.

A few weeks after our road trip, En showed me a picture on her phone. She'd taken it in a restroom stall at school in March 2019, two months before she graduated. Someone had started an unofficial poll, titled "Tally if you H8 Paly." Beneath the prompt, the hashmark count was up to twenty-five.

She told me that someone had scrawled "Then leave" under the hash marks, but either it didn't fit in the frame or En chose not to include it.

Grievances

It's too warm and the street we're walking on has nothing interesting to look at and there are loud cars whizzing by and what is even the point of all this walking when we could have had coffee at the hotel or even at that first place we looked at?

En doesn't actually say any of that, but I can guess that's what she's thinking. Her resentment hangs over us like a dark cloud. She ignores my conversational overtures and responds monosyllabically to my mother's. My mother and I make a show of bantering as though nothing is wrong, but I can feel the morning sliding sideways, our forced gaiety breaking against En's hostile silence.

I want to remind En how much she loved walking as a child, to say, *Remember how determined you were to walk all the way to that playground?* But I stop myself, because whenever I've brought that up before, En rolled her eyes at me and said, "God, Mom, can you *not?*" Even now she looks at me and says, "*Don't* bring up how I walked all the way to that playground from Babushka and Dedushka's apartment" even though I haven't said a word, and I spread my hands out to indicate that I wasn't planning on it.

It's true. I wasn't planning on it. She is no longer that three-year-old and I'm no longer that . . . what? What am I not?

Penelope

Greek mythology in a nutshell: men who leave and women who weave. The Fates–Clotho, Lachesis, and Atropos–spin and measure and cut. Penelope, Odysseus's loyal wife, holds off scores of grasping suitors for years by weaving a burial shroud for her father-in-law by day and unraveling it every night.

The only kind of weaving my mother and I have ever done was a brief foray into making latch hook rugs when I was in eighth grade. We sat on our living room couch for hours, knotting precut lengths of brown and tan and orange and yellow yarn through a canvas backing that, when finished, depicted a desert sunset. Filling row after row with knotted wool made me feel industrious and useful. *This must have been what women did in the olden days*, I thought, *this companionable sitting together, the busy hands, the ebb and flow of conversation.* My father quoted the opening lines of *The Tale of Tsar Saltan* when he saw us at work–"Three fair maidens, late one night, / Sat and spun by candlelight." Never mind that there were two of us, not three. Never mind that the women on my mother's side of the family can't sit still for very long. We're not adept with our hands. We're not patient enough, not careful enough. Too restless.

Whenever Grandma Ester talked about my father or about Grandma Tsilya, she would say, "*U nikh zolotyye ruki*"–they have golden hands. There was nothing they couldn't mend or put in order. Grandma Tsilya's small hands were veined, her knuckles gnarled, her nails short. After a lifetime of working with tools, the pads of my father's fingers are worn down to the point where he has almost no discernible fingerprints. Is that what it takes to leave a mark on the world–to wear your hands down in the service of others?

On my mother's side, I come from people who are melodramatic and attention-seeking, unreliable and impulsive. Perhaps that's how writers are, or how writers get made. I can't stitch evenly, but I can spin a yarn. Weave, embroider, embellish.

Material

En is ostentatiously lagging behind me and my mother, her displeasure palpable. "I don't think I've ever not liked walking," I say louder than necessary. I'm speaking to my mother but hoping En will hear me, hoping that my words will somehow dispel her bad mood. "Do you remember how we used to go on an after-dinner walk when we lived in Sunnyvale?"

Our route was usually the same, and we followed it almost every night: down quiet, wide Inverness Way past Ortega Park, right at Blackhawk Drive, another right at Dunholme Way, which brought us back home. The route was a rectangle with a roughly three-mile perimeter. Because not many of our neighbors took nighttime walks, the three of us had the quiet streets lined with single-story houses to ourselves, and I was irresistibly drawn to the life-sized dioramas behind the lit-up windows. The exposed inside of each house was its own little world–kitchens set up this way or that, or formal dining rooms, or a bright orange couch, or a couple watching TV side by side. If my mother caught me looking, she'd say it was rude to look through people's windows, and I would retort that people who didn't want other people to look into their houses should pull their curtains.

I turn back to En to tell her that her grandmother used to scold me for looking in people's windows when really, I was just observing, but En is looking down at her feet, and she refuses to look up. I turn to my mother and say, "Obviously, I was gathering material for my future career as a writer," and my mother smiles, and apropos of nothing, asks me if I remember San Marino.

I do remember San Marino. My parents and I went there in late December of 1977, during the tour of Italy my parents financed by selling the contents of our fourth suitcase at the Mercato Porta Portese. San Marino is a microstate–one of the smallest sovereign countries in the world, surrounded entirely by Italy–and we walked its nearly deserted streets, bundled up against the cold, marveling at how small it was, and how old, and how hilly, taking in the stone buildings, the narrow alleyways, the sweeping views from the ramparts.

"You probably don't remember this," my mother says, "but when it started getting dark, we passed a house with uncurtained windows, and there was a family around a table, talking and laughing, and there was all this food on the table–a roast, I think, and bread, and roasted vegetables. Carrots, potatoes." Her voice softens, grows wistful. "I remember thinking how cozy it looked, how warm."

En continues to seethe silently.

I can feel my jaw tightening. I want to tell En she's ruining the last day of our trip, that if I could go on nightly walks with my parents, she can walk a mile and a half to get coffee with her mother and grandmother. (Then I remember: I was a pliant Soviet child, and she is not.)

Unkind words roll around in my mouth, pressing to be let out. I want to tell En to get over herself. I want to tell my mother–who hasn't done anything wrong, who is just trying to lighten the mood–that there was no way she could have seen what was on the table in that lit-up room in San Marino in such detail without pressing her face up against the glass. But I don't. I bite the words back. En never said she wanted to go on a long walk to get coffee. My mother is pressing her face up against the glass of memory, and what she sees there is real to her. Who am I to question its veracity? I was nine years old when this happened, or didn't happen; all I knew at the time was that I had no school, that my parents and I were together, that each day was a grand adventure. I didn't know that we didn't have a home. I didn't care that we didn't have a home. My parents would figure everything out, I was sure of it.

Just then, my phone announces that we've arrived at our destination, which is called Paso Market Walk and not "super cute mini-mall."

Momentum

I may as well admit it: I've been jealous of Vladimir Nabokov for a long time. He was brilliant and sophisticated and cosmopolitan and curmudgeonly in exactly the way I wanted to be. He made of his exile a thing of beauty. It seemed singularly fitting that he died in the summer of 1977, two and a half months before my parents and I boarded a plane in Moscow's Sheremetyevo Airport and left Soviet Russia forever.

Nabokov was born on April 22–Shakespeare's birthday–in a lavish art nouveau mansion in the heart of Saint Petersburg. His family was cultured, wealthy, aristocratic, progressive; he grew up speaking English, Russian, and French with equal fluency. The family summered at a splendid ancestral estate in the nearby countryside. And then the Russian Revolution put an end to it all.

When Nabokov was seventeen, he and his family fled Saint Petersburg, first to Crimea, then to Athens. He attended Cambridge University and settled in Berlin, among almost half a million displaced Russian aristocrats, politicians, intellectuals, poets, artists, and writers. In 1922, Nabokov's father, a prominent champion of a Russian constitutional democracy, was assassinated by Russian right-wing monarchists. The bullet that felled him was meant for someone else–Russian historian and liberal politician Pavel Milyukov–but after the elder Nabokov wrestled the first assassin to the ground, the second shot him at point-blank range. The following year, Nabokov met Vera Slonim, a young Russian-Jewish woman who became his wife. In 1937, the couple moved to Paris; in 1940, after nearly a year of desperate maneuvering, Nabokov managed to secure a refugee visa to the United States, and in May of that year, he, Vera, and their young son Dmitri boarded the SS *Champlain* in Le Havre. The ship struck a German mine while returning to France; less than a month after that, France surrendered to Germany. Nabokov's brother Sergei, who remained in Paris, died in a Nazi concentration camp.

Many years later, Nabokov told an interviewer that he had propelled himself out of Russia so vigorously, with such indignant force, that he had been rolling on ever since. Apart from a country estate he inherited from his uncle in 1916–only to lose it a year later to the Bolshevik requisition of private property–he never owned a house. When he was a child, his mother impressed on him the importance of taking in and retaining the details of the world around him–the slant of light in the evening, the taste of wild strawberries, the smell of northern pine. This lesson stayed with him; in *Speak, Memory*, Nabokov evokes the places and sounds and smells of his perfect childhood with a hallucinatory clarity, reveling in what he calls the unreal estate of memory, the beauty of intangible property.

In the United States, Nabokov moved from one teaching stint to another (Wellesley, Cornell), and he and Vera and Dmitri moved from one rental to another. In the summers, the Nabokovs traversed the North American continent in search of butterflies (Nabokov was a devoted lepidopterist)–by Nabokov's own estimate, approximately 150,000 miles between 1949 and 1959. His treks took him to Tennessee, Texas, Arizona, Wyoming, California, Pennsylvania, Massachusetts. He traveled light, with a butterfly net and index cards on which he wrote the early drafts of his most celebrated novels.

Nabokov never learned to drive, and it was Vera, much like the stoic Mrs. Adams in *Roadside America*, who drove him uncomplainingly over mountain passes and prairies, through all kinds of terrain and all kinds of weather. Vera interceded when Nabokov tried to burn an early draft of *Lolita* in a backyard bonfire. She typed up his manuscripts, then retyped revised versions. She carried a handgun in her handbag. She did not leave after discovering that her husband had an affair while she was pregnant with Dmitri. She was clever and patient and loyal and steadfast, like Odysseus's wife Penelope, but with a driver's license and a concealed carry permit. If Vera harbored resentment about the affair or about giving up her own nascent writing career to become her husband's muse, chauffeur, secretary, and editor, she never voiced them.

Nabokov has fallen out of fashion. So has Henry James. When I was in graduate school, I was asked more than once why I was writing my dissertation on two dead white guys. No one seems to care much about nineteenth-century manners, the implications of what it means when a man sits while a woman stands. *Lolita*'s scandalous success has calcified into barbed suspicion, and I get raised eyebrows when I try to explain that *Lolita* is not an endorsement of pedophilia. I know only a handful of people who have read *Pnin* and *Pale Fire*, exquisitely wrought novels shot through with nostalgia and loss, novels that ensured Nabokov's place in the American literary canon and a comfortable retirement at a luxurious lakeside hotel in Switzerland.

It's not Nabokov's privilege I'm jealous of. I'm jealous of how lightly he traveled, of how little he seemed to need things. Private property, real estate–the things my parents and my husband and I worked so hard to acquire–meant nothing to him. I'm jealous of his perfectly calibrated nonchalance, his ability to keep rolling. He gathered no moss. There's an art to maintaining that kind of momentum, to holding things neither too tightly nor too loosely.

As advertised

My friend Debbie was right: The pastries are delicious, the coffee is delicious, the latte art is stunning. En regains her good cheer as soon as she gets her oat milk latte, a perfectly rendered oak leaf in the foam. She tells us she's been practicing her latte art, but she's still in the formless blob stage, whereas the barista here clearly knows what she's doing.

Housekeeping

Grandma Ester was restless and histrionic, Grandma Tsilya was a quiet homebody, but they were both fiercely loyal. They would do anything for any of us. They stayed home, took care of grandchildren, cooked and cleaned and worried, day after day, month after month, year after year. They kept the house in order.

In 1998, shortly after Orion was born, Aunt Klara had a massive stroke in the kitchen of her small apartment. My father and Uncle Boris headed to the emergency room to be with her and dispatched me to the apartment to help Uncle Isaak. I found him sitting at the oilcloth-covered kitchen table, a cup of cold tea before him. There were four bowls on the table: flour, sugar, three eggs, a stick of butter. "She was making you a birthday cake," he said, eyebrows raised high on his forehead in a kind of hurt bewilderment. "And then she just fell."

It was the day before my thirtieth birthday. I made Uncle Isaak another cup of tea and asked him if he'd eaten anything, and he said he wasn't hungry. We sat at the kitchen table for a while, and then I walked through their apartment picking up gauze, tourniquet bands, electrode pads. I wanted the apartment to be tidy. I could imagine how cozy it had been, how comforting–the orderly parade of cake ingredients, the cup of steaming tea on the table–before the blood vessel in Aunt Klara's brain burst and made everything dark.

I don't know why I was surprised that the paramedics left a mess in Aunt Klara and Uncle Isaak's apartment, considering what they were there for. The paramedics who saved En didn't clean up either.

I didn't know that they didn't clean up because I rode in the front seat of the ambulance that took En to the hospital after she almost died. It was two weeks into quarantine, and when the paramedics burst through our front door I thought, irrelevantly, *Nobody except paramedics can see the inside of people's homes anymore.* It was David who cleaned up the aftermath. He had been on a run in a nature preserve near our house and came home to find the oxygen tubing and gauze and electrode pads and paper wrappers.

In the ambulance, the driver told me it was lucky I was home, because another minute or two and En would have been gone. *If you're not home, you're in danger.* I didn't answer, because I was going to go for a walk that afternoon but changed my mind at the last minute, and I couldn't get my mouth to form the word "Yes," so I just nodded.

Backstitching

I did not dress to Grandma Tsilya's liking and I could never replicate the evenness of her stitches, but she did impress on me the importance of *zakrepka*, which means to fasten or to secure, even for something as basic as sewing on a button. In sewing, securing involves either backstitching over a completed row of stitches or making a loop at the end of the row and bringing the needle and thread through that loop, pulling the thread taut to make sure the stitches don't unravel. Both options entail a looping back, a return.

Accidents of birth

We all come into the world by accident, my father had said—my father, who was born three months before Nazi Germany invaded Soviet Russia. The nursery at the hospital where he was born was full of baby boys, and one of the nurses told Grandma Tsilya that all those boys meant a war was coming.

Orion and En were born into a different kind of war zone. David and I had declared war on autism because we wanted Nemo to be sovereign and independent and even though we were all fighting on the same side, we were nevertheless fighting, and when we weren't fighting, we were about to fight, and there were long stretches of time during which it seemed that the only time the fighting stopped was when we collapsed into bed at the end of each day. And even though Nemo had come so far, had accomplished so much—he graduated from high school, he went to college, he was a resident assistant in his dorm—there was a constant drumbeat of worry that something would go wrong, and in his junior year of college, something did: He developed severe depression, he began talking about wanting to end his life, he refused to take a medical leave and get help, he yelled at David and me over Skype and blamed us for making him this way, and this went on for months. The anguish, the pleading, the shouting, the not knowing. En was fifteen at the time. What did we miss over the months and years that it took him to regain his equilibrium? At what point did we realize that we were fighting a war on multiple fronts?

En left for the South Pacific in the fall of 2019. When I looked her up on Google Maps, it occurred to me that she had chosen to go as far from home as possible, which should not have surprised me but did.

Infidelities

At a bakery near the coffee place, we buy a dozen cupcakes to bring back to the men waiting for us at home. Then we walk back to the Marriott, side by side this time, and discuss infidelity.

There is so much infidelity in *The White Lotus*. Of the three generations of men vacationing together, two–the grandfather and the father–are serial adulterers. Ethan and Harper, the newly rich couple, discover that Cameron and Daphne, the couple they're vacationing with, are unfaithful to each other, and mistrust begins to seep into their own marriage. Tanya suspects that Greg is in love with someone else.

My mother mentions that shortly before he died, my grandfather was unfaithful to Grandma Ester. En stops walking and says, "What!" Exclamation point, not a question mark.

I've heard about my grandfather's infidelity before–and about Grandma Ester's convulsive rages after she discovered the affair–but En wants details. Who was this woman? How did they meet? Questions I never thought to ask. I don't even know her name.

They met at work, my mother says. And adds, "All I can tell you is that my parents got married very young. My mother was seventeen; my father was twenty. Then the war started. They lost a child; they lost their families. Babushka would have these outbursts–" My mother waves her hand, shorthand for screaming, tears, threats to kill herself.

The word for such outbursts in Russian is *skandal*, which sounds like "scandal." *Ustroit' skandal* means to make a scene. That was what living with my grandmother was like–one *skandal* after another, always coming out of the blue, always dissipating as though it never happened.

"Your grandfather was exhausted," my mother says. "He did whatever he could to get along with her, to shield me and your aunt from–" She gestures vaguely again. "He told me about the affair after it was over. 'I just wanted to be with someone quiet. I wanted some peace,' he said."

There's a long silence, and then En asks, "What was her name? The lady's?"

"Her name was Valentina," my mother answers.

"And when did you say the affair was? Approximately?" I ask.

My mother gives me a strange look. "The early '70s, I think? He died in 1975, so a year or so before that. Why?"

Until that moment, I had not known the name of the woman with whom my grandfather had a short-lived affair. But I do know this: For a brief period of time, when I was four or five, I had an imaginary friend whose name was Valentina. This would have been right around the time of my grandfather's affair. I remember, vaguely, a comforting, reassuring presence I talked to at night. Mostly, she just listened. I didn't make up her name; I just knew she was named Valentina. She appeared one day, and then she was gone.

"Oh, wow," En says, and I say, "I know," and my mother just shakes her head, not in denial but to underscore that of course, that tracks, because we are all a little bit woo-woo, the three of us.

"And, you guys, their first baby. Valeriy," I say.

"Babushka called him Valik," my mother says, and I make a mental note to check later whether the names Valeriy and Valentina are related. (They are: Both derive from the Latin *valens*, which means healthy and strong.)

We're almost back at the Marriott when my mother suggests that since there's no particular hurry to get on the road, we probably have time for at least one more episode of *The White Lotus*–maybe even two, so we can finish the whole season. We can ask for a late checkout, she says, and we do, and the clerk says we have until 1 p.m., which will get us through at least one episode. "Let's fun," we all say in unison, and En cackles her witchy cackle, and we go into my mother's room and pull the curtains against the daylight.

In "Abductions," the penultimate episode of the second season, three generations of the Di Grasso men–lecherous grandfather, philandering son, self-proclaimed nice guy grandson–track down their distant relatives in a remote Sicilian village. They expect a warm welcome, but the long-lost relatives–three generations of women living in placid self-sufficiency–greet them first with indifference, then with an angry stream of invectives, and finally with a kitchen knife. The grandmother brandishing the knife screams in Italian, "Get out! We don't know you!"

We don't know you

In graduate school, I studied the Russian formalists–a group of scholars and critics focused on examining how literary works are made and the specific literary devices that went into their making. One such device was *ostraneniye*, a Russian word that means to make foreign, to take familiar objects and concepts and put them in unexpected, unfamiliar contexts.

To be estranged from someone is to make the familiar strange. For many years, Grandma Ester was estranged from her brother Kolya, my cousin Masha's grandfather, because–well, no one is sure because of what, exactly. All I know is that Kolya might have done something or said something. Or maybe he didn't do something. And because one thing leads to another, I didn't meet Masha or her parents until 2022, long after Grandma Ester and my great-uncle Kolya were gone.

Grandma Ester was not a reliable narrator. She had said things about Kolya that turned out to be partly true but also not true. She pitted people against each other. There were long-standing grievances on her side of the family whose origins no one knew. When I asked my mother how many of Grandma Ester's brothers survived the war, she didn't know, because Grandma Ester was not on speaking terms with several of them.

I want to be very clear that Grandma Ester never wished anyone ill. That was just how she was.

This is how estrangements happen. A snag becomes a snare. A crack becomes a chasm. A thread breaks, or a clothesline, and by the time you notice it's too late to do anything about it. The train is already disappearing into the distance. "I don't know you anymore," you say to someone, or maybe you don't say anything, just let the silence grow.

Family therapy

En's first full sentence when she was a baby was "Do it by self." Unlike Nemo and Orion, she spoke early. She wrote and illustrated stories in elementary school. She was fiercely independent. She tracked down things Nemo and Orion lost–retainers, homework assignments, stray socks. She made it her job to look out for her brothers, to be the easy one.

I wrote earlier that En and I have a vexed relationship because mothers and daughters are complicated, and that's true. But our relationship was also complicated because she decided that she had to be the easy one, the responsible one–even though no one had asked her to be either of those things–and then, when she couldn't be the easy one, she told herself that she had ruined our lives, and meanwhile, David and I believed that we had ruined her life. Had ruined all three children's lives, in fact. We went around and around, arguing about who did or said what, or didn't. The same argument we had had with all of our children–same structure, different details. We argued about velocity and destination and distance–who should be going where, and doing what, and how soon–and we always ended up exactly where we started, but always expecting a different result, which is the very definition of stupid.

"Then leave," Grandma Tsilya had said to my father, but we didn't know how.

We spoke, separately and together, with earnest and well-meaning therapists, almost all of whom En loathed because she has the blessing and the curse of being able to spot insincerity instantly. While En was out of the room, one of the therapists suggested that we were all on a *journey*–so many of the therapists we spoke with used journey as a metaphor that I began to wonder whether there was a handbook somewhere with recommended phrasing for struggling families. David and I, she said, were farther along on our family's journey, and En was still at the starting point, and instead of waiting for her to catch up we might consider going back and meeting her and I thought, *Oh hell no, we're not doing that.*

Recently, I told En about that conversation. I wanted to show her that I understood how wrong David and I were, that instead of waiting for her to catch up we should have gone back and met her where she was. I wanted her to be proud of my insight, of how far I'd come. Instead, she narrowed her eyes and said, "Okay, two things: One, she said that because she could tell that you and Dad are overachievers and you'd appreciate hearing how far ahead you were, and two, who says we're on the same journey?"

Meeting halfway

Throughout the 1980s, Grandma Ester and Grandma Tsilya both lived in Belmont–Grandma Ester with my aunt and Grandma Tsilya with my uncle. Their houses were about three miles apart, and every so often, the grandmothers would call each other to borrow an onion, or a cup of flour, or a couple of eggs. They would designate a specific time to leave their houses and meet midway for the handoff. I like imagining their days punctuated by these meetings. I wonder if they recognized each other from far away, waved once the familiar outline came into view.

A math problem: A train leaves the station in the summer of 1941. A car pulls out of a driveway in the winter of 2023. If they are traveling toward each other at a constant speed across multiple generations and two continents, is it possible that they will ever meet?

Outerwear

When my parents met for the first time, on a long-ago snowy day in Moscow, my mother was wearing a winter coat made of rabbit fur dyed to look like mink. My father claims it was the ugliest coat he had ever seen.

We're less than a hundred miles from home, driving through Salinas Valley and discussing coats because it's overcast and En says she wants a long, sweeping black coat, like something Anna Karenina might wear. Or a chic New Yorker. I tell her that we're obviously related, because I have been on the hunt for exactly such a coat for years. Because I'm five feet tall, finding anything that doesn't make me look like two children in a trench coat is a challenge. En, who is two inches taller than me, says "OMG, same!"

My mother is still on the subject of the coat she was wearing when she and my father met. "I don't know why he hated that coat so much," she says, and then tells us how she and Grandma Ester fought bitterly over clothes when she was growing up. Grandma Ester insisted on buying clothes for my mother–I wondered briefly if she had said, "*Takovo u tebya nyet*" ("Like this, you do not have") to her–and my mother hated everything Grandma Ester brought home. Finally my grandfather convinced my grandmother to give my mother some money and let her get whatever she wanted.

My mother had a friend whose older sister worked as a seamstress in a factory. My mother paid her to sew her a coat, kelly green, nipped at the waist, a full skirt, crisp lines, giant pale green buttons. "I felt so regal whenever I wore it," my mother says, and sighs.

The worn-out green coat had been retired or given away by the time she and my father met, and my father asked her to have coffee even though he claims to have loathed the dyed rabbit-fur coat.

The rabbit-fur coat was followed by another coat, which my mother was wearing when we left the Soviet Union. The coat was an unremarkable cloth coat, but a few weeks before our departure, my mother bought two sable pelts with Grandma Ester because my parents had extra money from turning their apartment over to new tenants and we were allowed to leave with no more than fifty dollars per person. Grandma Tsilya, who had come from Odesa to say goodbye, sewed the sables onto my mother's coat collar with her usual care.

As we were preparing to board the plane, a border guard tilted his head, indicating for us to step to the side. He fingered the sable collar on my mother's coat and yanked, hard. The collar came off. "*Na zhivuyu nitku*," he said gleefully.

"*Na zhivuyu nitku*" means the stitching is provisional–that something is tacked or basted on before being permanently attached. The literal translation is "on a live thread," presumably because a live thread can be killed, or torn. "Contraband," the border guard added.

We were surrounded by KGB agents dressed in identical white shirts and black suits. Several men took my father away. My mother could see passengers boarding, and then everyone was on the plane, and she and I were standing there, and my father was still gone. When she asked where he was, the men surrounding her smirked.

After a time–minutes? Hours? My mother doesn't remember–my father reappeared, disheveled and angry. We boarded. The plane took off.

Foreshadowing

I'm driving as fast as I reasonably can because we're eager to return and equally eager to watch the season finale of *The White Lotus*. It's sunny when we leave Paso Robles, overcast in Salinas Valley, and now, as we drive through Gilroy, a light drizzle begins to fall, but nothing like the torrential rain and wind two days before. Has it only been two days? It feels both very long and very short.

En and my mother agree. We've done so much and seen so much–"Much have I seen and known," says Tennyson's Ulysses–but there's still the finale to watch, which means the trip won't really be over until we've all seen how the show ends.

My mother and En keep circling around the two couples vacationing together. Did Harper, Ethan's wife, sleep with Cameron, Daphne's husband? Was Daphne hinting to Harper that her children were not Cameron's? En says she still thinks Ethan has serial killer vibes, even more so now that she has seen six episodes. All three of us agree that the Di Grasso men are problematic; the grandfather is gross, the dad is obviously a sex addict, and the grandson, who proudly calls himself a feminist, is not–in spite of his claims to the contrary–a friend to women.

We also agree that there's something undeniably ominous about the palazzo where the high-end gays live, particularly at night, particularly with firepits illuminating its yawning courtyard and casting sinister shadows across the faces of the sculptures. "I don't trust those gays," En says, and because I can't stand it any longer, I say, "Do you see why it's reminding me of Henry James? The expatriates!"

My mother catches on immediately, because she has read *The Portrait of a Lady* and *The Wings of the Dove* and *The Golden Bowl.* She knows about James's expatriates–ambiguous, opaque, scheming. She understands that their dual allegiances allow them to have one foot in each world, to take advantage of others. In this calculus, rich, naive Tanya–who asks for an Oreo cake for breakfast, whose fantasy of Italy is to dress up like Monica Vitti and eat spaghetti with clams–is not going to fare well.

"Now I'm really worried about Tanya," my mother says.

"Don't worry about Tanya, Babushka," En replies. "I'm not sure who's going to die, but I'm positive it's not going to be Tanya. Tanya's a survivor."

Homecoming

Odysseus returns to Ithaca disguised as an old beggar, unrecognizable to all but his faithful dog, Argos; his loyal swineherd, Eumaeus; his childhood nurse, Eurycleia; and his son, Telemachus. Still in disguise, he makes his way to his palace, strings his bow—the bow none of the suitors could string—and massacres the suitors, one by one. Then he orders the maids who slept with the suitors to clean the blood and the gore, and once they're finished he tells Telemachus to hack them apart with his sword. Telemachus decides to do one better: He will hang them like doves, "or larks in the springes triggered in a thicket, / where the birds think to rest—a cruel nesting."

I have always hated this part of the *Odyssey*. Slaughter the suitors? Yes, please, absolutely. They are boorish and greedy and insufferable. We hate them from the beginning; we pull for Odysseus, especially after he returns and the suitors scorn and insult him in his guise as a beggar. When I taught the *Odyssey* in graduate school, one of my fellow teaching assistants compared Odysseus's pre-massacre speech to the suitors to something Rambo might say before going on a rampage:

> You yellow dogs, you thought I'd never make it
> home from the land of Troy. You took my house to plunder,

twisted my maids to serve your beds. You dared
bid for my wife while I was still alive.
Contempt was all you had for the gods who rule wide heaven,
contempt for what men say of you hereafter.
Your last hour has come. You die in blood.

You die in blood. So good. They had it coming. They deserve it. Fuck yeah. Devouring Odysseus's cattle, drinking his wine, profaning his house, bidding for his wife, twisting his maids to serve their beds–unforgivable offenses, all. And yet the maids are strung up one by one, "yanked high in air, / to perish there most piteously." Their feet dance a little, but not long. Even though they helped Penelope unweave the shroud. Even though they spied on the suitors.

But that's life, isn't it? Arbitrary and unfair. We all know that bad things happen to good people, or to mostly good people. Are the maids good? We don't know. They're not central to Odysseus's journey.

In 2005, Margaret Atwood wrote *The Penelopiad*, in which Penelope tells her side of the story. The twelve murdered maids serve as a chorus. They are furious and bitter, understandably so. They chant, "We had no voice / we had no name / we had no choice / we had one face / one face the same / we took the blame / it was not fair."

In Atwood's telling, Penelope is long dead; she is speaking to us from the underworld. "Now that I'm dead I know everything," she says. She wants to set the record straight. She doesn't want to be an edifying legend. She regrets turning a blind eye to her husband's slipperiness, his wiliness, his unscrupulousness. She regrets not speaking up for the maids. "I kept my mouth shut," she says. "I didn't contradict, I didn't ask awkward questions, I didn't dig deep. I wanted happy endings in those days, and happy endings are best achieved by keeping the right doors locked and going to sleep during the rampages."

"My tongue is my enemy," Grandma Ester used to say. Atwood's Penelope says, "It's a wonder I had any tongue left, so frequently had I bitten it over the years."

I have decided not to bite my tongue.

Just one quick thing

We return before dinner. My father and David and Orion greet us at the door. The house is warm and cozy and exactly as we left it fifty-four hours earlier, and yet we're changed in a way we can't put into words. By "we," I mean me, my mother, En, not the six of us, although for all I know, my father and David were also changed during our absence. But I'm talking about the women in our group. The ones who left.

I put the cupcakes on the kitchen counter and David tells me he got frozen dumplings from the Chinese place on El Camino and then my father asks how the drive back was and I tell him it was great, far less nerve-racking than the drive there, and my mother tells him again how well I drove and how calm I was, and David asks if we had fun and we say yes. We had fun. "Let's fun!" we could have said, but no one would have understood us. We have our own vernacular now.

Then, as politely as we can, we tell the gathered men that we have something very important we need to do, just real quick, and we go into the study.

We could have easily watched the last episode of *The White Lotus* on the family room TV, but that's not even a possibility that occurs to us. We need to be together one last time, just the three of us, me in the middle with my laptop, the ululating theme music of the opening sequence–which En refuses to skip, even when time is of the essence–pulling us together, pulling us in.

Spoiler alert

The second season of *The White Lotus* ends exactly as it had to end, with the characters behaving exactly as they were foreordained to behave. It's apparent to me what has to happen, but then again, I'm watching it for the second time.

When the inevitable happens, it's impossible not to rail against fate, even as you know railing will do no good. And so, after Tanya dispatches the murderous gays in the way that only Tanya could–clumsily, hysterically, chaotically, improbably–and then tries to climb over the yacht railing to the dinghy far below, En can't help but scream at the screen, even as the inevitable is inevitably unfolding. "Jump into the water, idiot!" En yells. "OMG, just *jump*! Like the other guy! Why are you climbing? Or at least take off your stupid shoes–" And it's right at this moment that Tanya loses her balance and plummets, gold stilettos, diaphanous dress, and all, striking her head on the side of the yacht, hard. *Thud. Splash.*

Full fathom five

The Tempest, Shakespeare's last play, opens with a terrible storm at sea. A ship is dashed on the rocks, the passengers are scattered about the island, a father mourns his drowned son, the son mourns his drowned father. But no–both are unharmed. Alonso is simply on one side of the island; his son Ferdinand is on another. They have been temporarily separated by the same magician who conjured the storm.

After my cousin Benji drowned, I dreamt that I found him at an airport; he wasn't dead, just lost. *Stop being sad, he's right here, I found him!* I wanted to shout to everyone. Then I woke up.

When Tanya falls overboard, the camera lingers on her billowing dress, her heavy earrings, her hair unfurling like a living thing. She looks like a creature from a myth. The tendrils, the strains of opera in the background, made me think of Ariel's song in *The Tempest*.

> Full fathom five thy father lies;
> Of his bones are coral made;
> Those are pearls that were his eyes:
> Nothing of him that doth fade,
> But doth suffer a sea-change
> Into something rich and strange.

Something rich and strange–such mournful, haunting beauty.

En is still fulminating. “I can’t believe it. I can’t believe I said she was a survivor! I can’t believe she didn’t think to take off her stupid shoes! She could have so easily climbed into the boat if she had just jumped overboard”–looking first to me, then to my mother, as though to convince us. My mother looks transfixed, like someone in a dream. “But is that not the most Tanya way to go?” I ask, and then I look down and see that the silver ring my father bought me in New York is still on my finger, but the celadon stone is gone.

Safe passage

There's something you need to know about my father: When he and my mother moved back to San Francisco, into an apartment on a hill with a view of the Golden Gate Bridge, he joined a rowing club. He rows regularly on the San Francisco Bay, where weather conditions can turn on a dime and where a person in a small rowboat can be flattened by a container ship or a ferry if he's not careful. He pilots open water swims, and he has pulled distressed swimmers from the water on multiple occasions. Once, a large halibut leapt into his boat–probably to avoid an even larger predator, he noted wryly–and he wrestled with the slippery, thrashing, quicksilver fish until he managed to heave it overboard.

A year after the pandemic began, Nemo found a teaching job in San Diego. He had regained his equilibrium, finished college, earned a teaching credential. He had been talking about wanting to move south for several years, but we didn't think he was serious. But he was, and now he had this job offer, and David and I did not want him to move over five hundred miles from home, to the other end of the state. He accused us of not believing in him, and we denied it, but there was no question that we were terrified. Something could go wrong. Something *would* go wrong. He had never lived in Southern California, or SoCal, as he called it. ("Nobody calls it SoCal," we told him, but he ignored us. It turns out that people didn't call it SoCal when we lived there, but now they do.) The traffic, the unfamiliar setting, the lack of support. He would end up in such a puddle. What kind of puddle, we weren't sure, but we knew it would be bad.

Both my mother and father took his side. "You can't protect him forever," my father said. "You have to let him live his own life."

"Fine," David and I said. "If he wants to move, we can't stop him." To Nemo we said, "It's your show. You figure it out."

My father volunteered to drive with him to San Diego and help him move into his apartment. He spent two days there, accompanying Nemo on IKEA and Target and Trader Joe's runs, helping assemble furniture, stocking the fridge. Two months later, my father drove four hundred miles to Orange County to pick up En, who had been adrift since the pandemic began, and drove her home. Eventually, En rented a room in a house in Cupertino and started taking community college classes and found work as a barista, and it was at the Cupertino house that my mother and I picked her up when we began our drive south.

The San Francisco Bay is big; my father's boat is very small. In addition to the halibut that leapt into his boat, he has encountered whales, sea lions, cargo ships, tourists who wave to him from tour boats, and on one occasion, two catamarans whose crews were training for the America's Cup race. The two catamarans came out of nowhere, side by side, bearing down on his boat at full speed. The team photographer snapped a photograph of that moment, my father's tiny boat, the looming catamarans, the choppy, dark green water, the white spray.

My father wrote about that encounter in the rowing club newsletter. He said his first instinct was to row as fast as he could, to get out of the way; then he realized that if he stayed put–became predictable, as he phrased it–the catamarans could use him as a mark and maneuver around him. The catamarans split apart at the last minute, leaving less than ten yards of room on either side of his boat.

In Greek myth, Charon is the ferryman who rows across the River Styx to bring the souls of the dead to the underworld. In return, he receives an *obol*–a small coin that serves as a bribe or a payment. The stone from my ring was not in the car, or in my purse, or in my suitcase. I looked everywhere–my pockets, the car floor, between the seats–but it was gone. Even invoking Saint Anthony didn't help.

I like to imagine that the stone is on the ground somewhere in Sensorio, lying quietly in a glimmering field that brightens as the sun sets. Or maybe it fell out on our last morning in Paso Robles, on the walk En hadn't wanted to go on. Or, and I think this is the most likely, it had to be lost, taken as some sort of payment to the gods who oversee travel and transit, a small token in return for keeping us safe.

TRIP ROUTE

Art by Zoey Powers

ACKNOWLEDGMENTS

Any journey entails trials and obstacles, thresholds, transformations, losses, and rewards. This is true of an epic voyage, a three-day road trip, and the process of putting one word after another to tell a story.

Invariably, as with any adventure, there are mentors and allies along the way. I'm fortunate to have benefited from extraordinarily generous mentors, allies, friends, and family members who helped bring this book into the world and into readers' hands.

Among them are Malcolm Harris, whose brilliant book *Palo Alto: A History of California, Capitalism, and the World* eloquently put words to something I've suspected for a long time: that Palo Alto, where I've lived for the past twenty-six years, is haunted. I'm indebted to Malcolm for his insights into the history of capitalism in California and particularly for his astute examination of the complicated legacy of Stanford University.

Caroline Grant's meticulous, attentive reading and insistence on regular check-ins was instrumental in helping me cross the finish line. Our collaboration is proof that a writing group doesn't have to be big to be effective, and I am deeply grateful for her friendship and her generous insights.

Laurie Filipelli and Elyse Fenton were among my earliest readers, and both of them detected the spark of something I couldn't yet name in the messy first pages I sent them. Thanks to their encouragement, that spark grew into something bigger than I could have imagined. What a gift to be part of a trio (or, as we like to call ourselves, coven) of women who understand language and words and stories so deeply and intuitively. Huge thanks to you both for lighting many, many lanterns as I wandered through the thickets.

Speaking of lanterns: Brooke Warner, thank you for being a bright light in your unstinting work to democratize and demystify publishing. Shannon Green, Lindsey Cleworth, Katherine Lloyd, and the talented team of editors, designers, and publishing wizards at She Writes Press, I am incredibly grateful for everything you do to usher a book from nebulous idea to stunning reality. And speaking of wizardry: I am forever indebted to Julie Coryell, publicist extraordinaire, whose talent for seeing possibilities where others see dead ends is nothing short of magical.

A standing ovation should go to Zoey Powers, who transformed vibes and a lot of hand-waving into a beautiful map. And to everyone who fed me, took me for walks, engaged in long discussions about untranslatable words and untranslatable feelings, sent memes and reels and words of encouragement: Thank you, thank you, thank you.

All citations from the *Odyssey* were taken from Robert Fitzgerald's translation.

The words of Osip Mandelshtam's 1915 poem "Insomnia. Homer" often beat a refrain in my head as I was writing–so much so that I wanted to use a line from the poem as an epigraph for this book. An epigraph is a small thing, but I struggled mightily to capture the cadence and piercing lyricism of Mandelshtam's verse until I stumbled upon Mark Pettus's brilliant translation.

At the heart of Mandelshtam's poem is the realization that everything in the world is set in motion by love–the sea, Homer, the thousand ships that set sail for Troy. As difficult as it was to translate his words from Russian to English and retain their magic, conveying the depth of my love and my gratitude to my parents, my husband, and my children is immeasurably more difficult. How can I fully thank my parents, whose courage propelled me to a different continent and a different life and who taught me how to be a person in the world? Or my husband–my true love, my first and last reader, and my compass, the person who shared his life with me even though I flung the first ring he gave me into the forest? Or my children, without whom the world would be a duller, flatter place? Everything I know about velocity, direction, time, distance, and momentum I learned from them.

ABOUT THE AUTHOR

Photo credit: Dean Birinyi Photography

Irena Smith is a college admissions expert and the author of the award-winning memoir *The Golden Ticket: A Life in College Admissions Essays*. Her obsession with how words work began early (as a child growing up in Soviet Russia, she was known to occasionally stand on furniture and recite Pushkin poems) and led to a PhD in comparative literature and a tendency to pepper conversations with literary references and disquisitions about the difference between "less" and "fewer." You can learn more at www.irenasmith.com or find her at @irenasmith on Substack, where she writes about parents and children, generational expectations, the petty indignities of middle age, and the importance of embracing a broader, more generous vision of what it means to succeed.

Looking for your next great read?

We can help!

Visit www.shewritespress.com/next-read
or scan the QR code below for a list
of our recommended titles.

She Writes Press is an award-winning
independent publishing company founded to
serve women writers everywhere.

SWP